The
Principal
Chronicles
Two/Too/II/As Well
by David Garlick

Story Illustrations by Lindsay Chasten

To Miss Bennea,

From the author who
caught the kite string.

Best regards

David Garlick

◆ FriesenPress

One Printers Way
Altona, MB R0G 0B0
Canada

www.friesenpress.com

ISBN
978-1-03-830634-0 (Hardcover)
978-1-03-830633-3 (Paperback)
978-1-03-830635-7 (eBook)

1. HUMOR, SCHOOL & EDUCATION

Distributed to the trade by The Ingram Book Company

Praise for
The Principal Chronicles

And for
The Principal Chronicles Two

Table of Contents

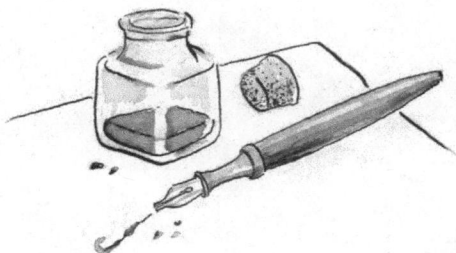

Writing Happens

It's a mistake to think of writing as what happens
only with pen in hand or keyboard to hand.
It also
happens as you try to clean red wine from a white dress,
hold a newborn baby,
or wipe the tears from a child's face.
It happens when you walk alone in a forest.
It happens the first time you hold a lover's hand.
It happens when you hug the boy whose dog's just died.
It happens when you laugh or cry with a friend.
Like life,
writing happens all the time.

Before the Beginning

Before you read the introduction to this book, it's important for me to thank a bunch of people and give you a few warnings or provisos.

First, the thanks: to my lovely and supportive wife: Linda is a character in a few of these stories, but she's actually in them all. She's the one that convinced me I could write these things, the one who laughs out loud in most of the right places, and the one who tells me, honestly, when I've missed the mark and to go back and try again.

There are a bunch of *real* names in this book, as there were in the first. If a name is real, I owe them a part of who I am today. I won't list them all here, as there are too many. You'll read them as you go through the book, but there are two who have passed on and won't be able to see their names in print: Paul Renaud and Bob Bellaire.

Then there are my beta readers, who are supportive and critical at the same time, offering suggestions and finding the occasional typo: Graham White, Darlene Chasten, Janette Long, Kathie Renaud, and my whole uni comm class; my Elder College class: Sue Lesa, Kevin McCabe, Kaye McMann, Peter Mudrack, Julie Rivait, and

Janet Romano; Anna Colledge, Dave Dekindt, my brother Ken, his wife Trish, Karen Demers, Gisele Seguin, and my cousin, Barb Hargreaves, as well as Doug and Jim McDowall and Doug Peterson. My parents are too, but all they ever say is that they're proud of me and that they like the stories—and for that they deserve special thanks.

It's interesting that, for my first book, Lindsay Chasten, my niece and its illustrator, was not a beta reader. She didn't read the stories until they were published. I simply asked her, for example, for a picture of a tornado. "You know, like in *The Wizard of Oz*, a big one, with a cow or a car in it." And she drew it for me. This book is different. She asked for the stories so she could see why I was asking for what I was asking and so became both the illustrator and a beta reader—all while also being an exploration geologist in South Dakota.

Now for the provisos:

- ✓ Any mistakes you find are mine.
- ✓ Please don't assume that everything in this book is true. I've written it like a memoir because *most* of it is true. Some of the material is only stuff I wish were true. Some is completely fictional. If you ask me, I'm happy to tell you which are which. My friend Dave Dekindt thinks that the fictional stories should have their own section, at the end, but I think they fit in better where they are. I like the fact that they could, or maybe should, be true.
- ✓ If you were actually there when the story took place and you think, "That's not the way I remember it," remember also that memory, both yours and mine,

can be faulty. If my way made you laugh, or makes anyone laugh, or makes them tear up, it's okay. If my way made you tell a friend your version, and you both laughed, or teared up, that's okay too. It's what I was trying to do.

✓ If you weren't there, and you say to yourself, "No . . . That can't be true!" but you laugh or tear up, guess what? That's all right too. But you're probably wrong.

Why I Wrote the Book
in the First Place

For many years, I traded stories with friends and colleagues at dinner parties, at the pub, and at staff meetings. "What's the most embarrassing thing that happened to you in your career?" "What's the best thing that happened to you this month?" "What's the funniest thing that's happened?" That kind of thing.

Good times. Good laughs.

No one ever asked, "What's the most depressing thing that ever happened?" "What's the worst thing that happened to you this year?" Bad things happened, and, if pressed, I can trade a few of those stories as well. Teaching isn't all fun and games. As a principal, I saw my share of bad things. But I don't dwell on them, and not much would be gained by telling those stories over a glass of wine and a fine dinner.

Near the end of my career, I got the idea of spending a good portion of the final staff meeting each year trading "Best stories of the year." I asked everyone to say something positive—funny—at our last meeting. If someone was stuck, I let them pass, but I always came back to them, and teachers knew I wasn't going to let them off the hook.

Everyone shared. The vast majority were eager and waiting to tell their story: the kid who finally got *it*, whatever *it* was; a memory from Buddy Week; the supportive phone call from a parent; the school team winning a game against the archrival. I don't remember what all else, but I do remember the feelings I had as teachers told their stories. I remember the laughter. I remember being thanked—and thanked a lot—after each of these meetings.

It was a fine way to end a year. Maybe one of the best ways.

So. Back when COVID started, and people were legitimately worried about the end of the world, and we were being held in thrall by all things Donald Trump, I found myself becoming a very angry and frustrated man. I shouted at the television. I shouted at my smart phone and the newspaper. I shook my fist at the world.

This wasn't normal for me. I'm known for my patience. Without exception, if kids heard me ranting in the hallways it was either a performance or a joke. I don't remember, ever, losing my temper with a teacher. But now I was *retired* and shouting at the world. And it wasn't an act. I was angry. I was frustrated. Like most people, I was scared and worried.

So one day, I sat down at my computer, but rather than yell at it, I looked through an old file I'd saved. "Barebones Incidents" it's called; hundreds of two or three sentence reminders of things that happened to me during my career. Many of them, things that made me laugh. As I read them again, I laughed again.

I began to expand some of them into short stories. As I finished each of them, I'd send them off to a small group of friends and family members. Their comments were all positive and said, basically, "Keep going, these are good!"

So I did. I wrote about fifty of them, and forty of them made it into *The Principal Chronicles*, which was published at the end of 2021.

The stories that were left out weren't bad. They weren't of poor quality. It was just that *The Principal Chronicles* was long enough, and some things had to be left out.

As soon as *The Principal Chronicles* was published, I began to be asked when a second collection would be written. That's what this is. The stories I'd left out weren't "seconds." They weren't damaged fruit. Most are here, as part of this collection. In thirty-three years of teaching, an awful lot will happen to a person. If you throw in their time in school and university, as well as their time in retirement, there will almost certainly be enough material for a second book.

So. Let me tell you another story . . .

Part One:
David as Student

The Day My Mother
Saved My Life

I remember the day my mother saved my life like it was yesterday. Well, that's not exactly true. To be honest, I remember very little about the actual day. It's better to say I remember her saving my life like it was yesterday. That's what stands out.

There wasn't anything particularly brave or heroic about what she did. She didn't, for example, race into a burning building to pull me out. She didn't run into traffic to push me out of the path of an oncoming transport truck. She didn't even cut my leg at the site of a rattle-snake bite and suck out the poison, though I'm certain she would have done all those things had they been necessary.

But she saved my life that day as surely as if any of those things had happened.

Mind you, this is the same woman who often threatened to "wring my neck like a chicken's" if she should come down there to the pantry and find the can of beans or the bag of onions I couldn't see. That happened fairly regularly. She was always going to wring my neck, or my brother's or my sister's.

I don't think she ever actually would have wrung any of our necks. At least she never did, and I know that I often gave her reason to. And she did, as I said, actually save mine—my neck, I mean.

I don't remember much about the actual day. It was a family picnic. We could have been on vacation in a park. We could have been at Niagara Falls. We could even have been in Alberta. We may just have been a few miles away from home at Point Pelee. It was sometime between 1966 and 1970.

It was definitely a beautiful, hot summer day. I'd been acting like the hyperactive six- to ten-year-old I was. I'd probably almost knocked over the barbecue. I'd probably not been watching where I was running and ran straight into the fender of our car, almost denting it. I'd probably tripped over something and nearly "taken my head off." And I'd probably picked on my little sister until she was crying, and so I had to be yelled at and told to just sit down for five minutes, okay?

Coupled with all or most of that, I'd almost certainly not had to go to the bathroom when we left home, or the camp site, or the motel, even though both my mother and my father would have told me to try. Fifteen minutes later, though, I would have had to go.

The reason I don't remember the day is that it was so typical.

As an aside, I just realized that although I told you my mother's regular threat of violence, I didn't tell you my father's. Whereas my mother was always going to wring somebody's neck, my father never specified what he was going to do. "One of these days, David Sidney . . ." (Adding the middle name indicated that *whatever* he was going to do, it was perhaps imminent.) "One of these days I'm gonna . . ." and then he left it to our imaginations. I used the pronoun "our" on purpose, because the threat was always made in the presence of both my siblings. To be clear, sometimes it was one of my siblings being threatened as well. Ken and Janice weren't perfect.

Anyway, on the day my mother saved my life I'd been acting the way I normally acted. I was exasperating. And not just to my parents. I'm certain that my older brother Ken had always had just about enough out of me. Since I often made my little sister Janice cry, I'm sure she'd had enough too.

Then, I must have done something extra. I cannot imagine what it was, because as I've said, everything I listed above was pretty much just normal, everyday stuff. I was the kid who drank the non-potable water after reading the sign telling me not to and spent the rest of that night throwing up outside our tent; I was also the kid who slid down the side of a mountain in Alberta and, quite literally, could have fallen to my death. So whatever it was that I'd done must have been pretty extreme.

"DAVID SIDNEY GARLICK!" (Note all three names, never heard before in anger.) "YOU SIT DOWN THERE RIGHT NOW AND BE STILL AND BE QUIET! I DON'T WANT TO HEAR SO MUCH AS A PEEP OUT OF YOU!" (No time limit specified.) "IF I DO, I WILL WRING YOUR NECK!"

My father had never made that threat before. Whereas I was pretty sure my mother would never follow through with it, I was equally certain that, if I *did* make a peep, my father would, indeed, wring my neck.

So I sat at the picnic table quietly. There was no point in crying, as that would probably count as a peep, as would asking if crying counted. My mother sat next to me, on my left, with my sister on my right. My father and brother sat across from us. Lunch was served, and I ate silently. I didn't even comment on how good anything was, as I was concerned that might also count as a peep.

I don't remember what we ate. Probably barbecued hot dogs and potato salad. I *do* remember the dessert: jarred peaches in syrup. I remember everything about them. I remember the jar, its label, and the gold colour of the lid. I remember the white paper plate and my mother spooning the peaches out of the jar and onto it. I remember their taste and eating them in complete silence, finishing before anyone else, and then sitting on my hands so that I couldn't accidentally do something with them to get myself killed. I also remember the wind coming up from behind me, and it very quickly sliding my almost empty plate, filled only with syrup now, across the table and onto my father's shirt and lap, sticking to his shirt.

It was like one of those moments in a Western cowboy movie. Everything stopped except for the wind. We sat as a sort of tableau, which lasted for both an eternity and only a few seconds.

I waited to have my neck wrung, certain it was about to happen, as was my brother. That *had* to count as more than just a peep. But then, my mother saved my life.

She didn't jump up and implore my father not to kill me. She didn't get between him and me.

She saved my life by laughing.

She has a wonderful and infectious laugh. Not a loud laugh, but one that clearly says she finds something funny and you should too. She laughed until my brother was laughing, and my little sister as well. My father didn't want to laugh, I could tell, but soon he couldn't help himself. It developed into that most rare kind of laugh that you have no control over and can't stop. And then we were all laughing. And no one was wringing anyone's neck.

What should have resulted in my quick death became instead a family story that's been told tens of times over the years.

The Day My Brother Really *Did* Save My Life

Although my mother didn't *really* save my life that day, because my father wouldn't *really* have killed me, when I read this story to her for the first time, after she'd finished laughing, she asked, "Do you remember when your brother really *did* save your life?"

I knew exactly what she was referring to.

Once, on a very similar kind of day—a hot and sunny, middle to late summer day—the five of us were in the family car, driving, I don't know, to the Corn Crib maybe? A place you could buy corn on the cob, cooked for you and dipped in salted butter. It was one of the best experiences of childhood.

Because it was a hot and sunny day, and this was before most cars had air-conditioning, we had the windows rolled down, and Ken had brought along his green plastic G.I. Joe–type canteen filled with water. He'd had to sneak it into the car, because my mother had told him not to bring it, thinking he'd spill the water all over the place. My father had given us each a piece of hard candy to keep us, well, probably just me, quiet. I was six, maybe seven, meaning Ken was eleven or twelve.

It was a great morning, and in most respects, it would have been completely forgettable, because this was just something we did as a family. Like the incident above, I only remember it now because my brother saved my life.

I *had* been keeping quiet. Ken hadn't spilled water all over the place. I hadn't even been bothering my little sister. And then Dad hit a bump in the road. My mother made the noise she did whenever she thought we were all going to be killed in traffic: a sharp intake of breath through gritted teeth. She made it once or twice every day we were in the car together, sometimes as we were pulling into our driveway.

None of us kids thought we were going to die, but whatever happened, it was a bit of a shock. I too made the same noise as my mother, but then I stopped making any noise at all. The hard candy my father had given me had been sucked down my throat and I was choking to death. Ken, to his credit, thought very quickly and offered me his canteen. It didn't help.

"Kenneth Garlick! Did you bring that canteen? I told you not to!" my mother snapped.

"Mom, David's choking. Dad, pull over!"

Neither my mother nor my father understood what was happening.

"David's going to spill water all over the place, and you're going to have to clean it up, young man. I told you not to bring that thing!"

I continued to choke, waving my arms. I forget if I actually spilled any water.

"Dad! Pull over!"

"You'd better do as your mom says, Ken. Put that canteen away."

"DAD! PULL OVER!"

I couldn't see myself, obviously, but Ken tells me my face had gone an interesting shade of purple-blue by the time my father pulled over. Ken jumped out of the car and ran around to my side, dragging me from the back seat. I don't know when or where he learned to do it, but he pounded me on the back, one, two, three times, until the hard candy shot out of my mouth and onto the gravel shoulder of the road we'd been driving on.

The first four or five breaths I took started by sounding very similar to my mother's reaction to us almost all being killed, sharp and long intakes of breath except my mouth was wide open, and I was breathing as deeply as I could. If a bug had been anywhere near me, I would have sucked it in and started choking again. But soon I calmed down. Ken reached into the car and passed me his canteen again.

"You okay now, David?" asked my very concerned father.

"Yes, sir. Pretty stupid of me."

"No more hard candy for you until you're twenty-seven!" said my mother. "And you, young man—" she said, addressing my brother. "You? You can bring that canteen with you whenever you want from now on!"

When my brother related his version of events to me just last week, filling in some of the blanks my mother and I had about the incident, he thought it hilarious, that we all just piled back into the car afterward and drove on to the Corn Crib, or Point Pelee, or wherever we'd been heading.

I'd almost died, and Ken had saved my life.

A pretty normal day, all things considered.

George Pierrot Presents: Dave Garlick Goes to Alberta and Becomes a Storyteller

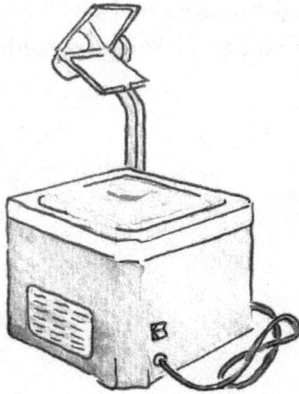

How does someone become a storyteller? I can tell you that, at least in my case, it's not inherited. My mother rarely tells stories, and though my father tries, he's pretty terrible at it. He's led an interesting life too, so it's too bad that he's not better at it. He doesn't seem to understand something that really would be interesting. For example, I was well into my forties before I'd even heard of Joe Gene, the One-Legged Salvation Army Man. How could you have a character with a name *that* good and never tell his story?

Apparently, speaking in front of a crowd is a huge fear for most people, almost as big as the fear of death. I don't *know* this, but I've heard it. I may even have read it somewhere, but I can't tell you where, so don't quote me, but public speaking is not something most people want to do.

Ever.

I became pretty good at it. Talking in front of a class became really easy for me. Talking in front of my staff too. Nothing to ever worry too much about. Graduations took more planning, but they were fun too.

Elementary school tried to prepare kids for it. Show-and-tell started, I think, in kindergarten and continued through to Grade 2. You'd bring something in from home, your favourite toy or book or something, and then you'd go to the front of the class and talk about it. To be honest, I don't remember ever doing it, but I must have. The fact that I don't remember anything tells me that it wasn't terrifying. I remember most terrifying stuff.

From Grade 4 through 8 there was current events. Every once in a while, you'd be responsible to read something from the local newspaper, cut it out, staple it to the current events board and talk about it. Again, I don't remember ever doing this, which is kind of weird given I must have had to do it at least a few times every year for five years. But, not terrifying at least, even if not memorable.

In Grade 7, we had to do actual speeches. Prepared things. Pages long. Mr. Cope did his best to calm and prepare us for this, but for some reason, this, a speech, was different.

"It's just five to fifteen minutes long. Introduction, body, conclusion. Say what you're going to say; say it; say that you said it. Simple," said Mr. Cope, sitting on an empty student desk at the front of the room. Tie loosened, sleeves rolled up to his forearms.

Mr. Cope was cool. A younger man, I don't know how old really. Kids never know such things. Thirty maybe? Almost thirty? Thinning hair, but even as an eleven-year-old, I knew it was premature and not his fault. My father explained that to me. Fred Cope was my first male classroom teacher.

"*Fifteen minutes*! I can't talk for fifteen minutes!" I said.

"Of course you can, David! I have a hard time *stopping* you from talking! But it doesn't have to be fifteen minutes. I said five *to* fifteen minutes." Mr. Cope was speaking to me, but for the benefit of the whole class.

"Does it have to be memorized?" asked Carla Meddins.

"Well, no, but I don't want you reading the thing either. There's nothing more boring than listening to someone read a speech. I don't want any of us to be bored."

The class had several more questions. Topics were up to us, but we had to get them approved by the teacher. We had two weeks to prepare. Rough drafts were encouraged but not required. We could use pictures if we liked. Slides? Yes. We could use the overhead projector if we wanted. We could even use the opaque projector!

A quick aside: You probably know what an overhead projector is, as well as a slide projector. You probably don't know what an opaque projector is. It looked ungainly. It was a big, grey metal thing with a glass lens about six inches in diameter. You could use it to project just about anything onto a screen at the front of the class! Books, paper, photographs—anything! Slide the stuff in at the bottom, adjust the focus, and presto! Maybe it wasn't that easy. I only ever saw one of the things. Maybe they were super expensive. Maybe they were dangerous and caught fire. I don't know. Anyway, we could even use the opaque projector!

I went home more excited than concerned. But then I had to come up with a topic. Everyone would choose the Apollo missions and landing on the moon. Everyone would also choose the Detroit Tigers. And the Beatles. So, of course, I chose all three of those and started work right away. I had books on the space race. I'd been to see the Tigers and had their pictures posted in my room. I had a picture book of the Beatles.

"David, if everyone is doing their speeches on the Beatles, the Tigers, and the moon landing, why are *you* doing those too?" asked my mother.

"Well, I know about them. I don't have to learn much. I just have to write the speech."

"But don't you think your audience will find it boring, listening to the same things from thirty different kids? I'd pick something that no one else is talking about."

"Like what?"

"You went to Alberta last year, camped for two weeks, fell down a mountainside, and could have died. Saw buffalo and prairie dogs . . ."

"And got sick from drinking water I shouldn't have . . ."

"Exactly! Now *that* stuff is interesting! You won't really have to write anything! Just pick a few photos and talk about them as you show them on the screen! Just like George Pierrot!"

I'm guessing you don't know who George Pierrot was. He had a Detroit-based TV show in the early to midsixties called *George Pierrot Presents*. It must have aired on Sundays, because I only remember watching it at my grandparents' home, and we often had Sunday dinner at their place. It was a travelogue show, and by today's standards, I'm sure it would be incredibly boring, but in the sixties, it was great entertainment. I don't know that Mr. Pierrot ever went anywhere interesting himself, but every week, he'd have a guest who *had* been somewhere interesting: Egypt or Paris or Colorado, maybe Alaska—always places I hadn't been yet. George and his guest sat in comfortable looking chairs with a projector screen behind them. For half an hour, they'd show slides, and the guest would talk about their travels. It never seemed scripted, just a conversation supported by black and white pictures. "Is that a water buffalo?" "Yes. Yes, it is! Did you know that they can be as dangerous as a lion? They look pretty peaceful, but you don't want to pet one!" George and his guest would laugh, the guest removing the cigarette from his mouth to do so, tapping the ash into the large crystal ashtray provided for that purpose.

And I would note that I should never pet a water buffalo.

I went through the hundreds of pictures my parents and brother had taken on our recent trip out west. "How many do you think I should take?" I asked my mother.

"How long are you going to talk about each one?"

"Depends. Some are just pretty. I don't have to say much at all. 'This is Lake Louise. This is Lake Louise too.' That kind of thing."

"Are you going to answer questions?"

"If anyone asks."

"Then I'd say no more than ten or fifteen."

In the same way I have very few memories of show-and-tell or current events, I have no memories of the speeches the other kids gave. I'm sure that most of them were at least okay, and that the Beatles were, in fact, the best band in history and the Tigers were going to win the World Series again. I also don't *really* remember my speech either. What I *do* remember is being really comfortable; kids laughing, asking questions, and applause at the end. Mr. Cope said, "That wasn't really a speech, Dave. But you did talk for fifteen minutes, and it was pretty entertaining. I guess it was . . . okay."

It hadn't impressed Mr. Cope. But in my mind, he wasn't the audience. The kids were my audience. Even at eleven years old, I knew how important it was to consider the audience. And so, on that day, I became a storyteller.

At the Intersection of Adolescence and Technology

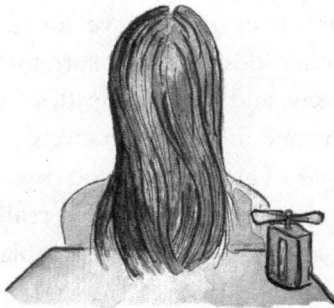

This is not a story about having to borrow the car from Dad or having it break down on a first date. This is not a story about trying to find a payphone far enough from home so as not to be embarrassed at calling a girl in front of my parents or siblings.

It is a story of the first intersection of technology and my own adolescence.

It's important for me to tell you at the outset that although I'd never met him, Roland Markham became a hero of mine in the late spring of 1968 when my brother came home from school to tell me that Roland, a student in his Grade 8 class, had turned his school desk into a crystal radio so he could listen to baseball games during class.

"Get out! You can't do that!" I exclaimed. Then, after a second, I added, "What's a crystal radio?"

"It's a radio that needs no batteries and you don't plug it in! Roland just needed a toilet paper roll, an eraser, some wire, and a few odds and ends from home and voilà! His desk became a radio! He's a bit of a geek, but I've gotta admit, it's pretty cool! Even Mr. Carruthers ended up thinking it was neat. He was angry at first though. He thought Roland had damaged the desk and was gonna send him to the office, until Roland convinced him to put the little earpiece into his ear. And just as he did, Al Kaline hit a double! Carruthers likes baseball, I guess. So Roland didn't get sent to the office. He just had to give us updates at the end of each inning."

I was eight. I consulted my brother's Boy Scout manual and saw that, yes, it was possible to turn a school desk into a radio. I didn't want to get into any trouble, and so looked into the possibility of making a crystal radio set at home. My parents were pleased at this foray into the realms of science and technology and so bought me a crystal radio kit. I put it together with minimal adult supervision and began listening to the one or two stations the radio picked up. Roland may have been a bit of a geek, as my brother said, but he'd turned an eight-year-old on to technology.

Adolescence has nothing to do with eight-year-olds, but it does have to do with twelve-year-olds. By the time I was twelve, I'd moved on from crystal radios but was still, or rather was now, fascinated with the simple technologies available to twelve-year-olds at Janisse's Hobby & Toy Store. Working model steam engines, which could operate a small drill or saw were too expensive for me, but the little motors that drove model automobiles were pretty *in*expensive, and if you took the red plastic propeller from an even less expensive balsa wood glider and glued it to the motor, you could make yourself a personal fan!

Which I did, and like Roland a few years before, I brought it to school.

Like I said, I was twelve. Grade 7. At the beginning of adolescence. As fascinated as I was with the technologies at Janisse's Hobby & Toy Store, I was even more fascinated by girls. Now, I'd always *liked* girls, all the way back to Helen Tapper in kindergarten. But now it was different. Now I was twelve and Bethany Langer was sitting in front of me.

I fell hard for Bethany almost from the moment I met her. She was new to our school that year, and when Mr. Cope read her name out for attendance, he said her last name, Langer, so it rhymed with "hangar."

"Excuse me, sir. It's pronounced 'Lahnjay,'" she said, correcting him. "It's French." I fell a little bit in love right then. I'd never met a French girl before.

She turned around in her desk to introduce herself to me. "My first name is Beth. Usually, when someone's named Beth, it's short for Elizabeth. But in my case, it's short for Bethany. I was named after my grandmother."

"Your grandmother's name is Bethany?"

"No, silly. It's Elizabeth." And then she laughed at me. A laugh that reminded me of many small bells. And I was gone.

I don't know that Bethany ever knew that I was in love with her. I certainly never told her. A twelve-year-old boy never tells a Bethany Langer that he's in love with her. Throughout that year, though, I tried to *convey* that I was in love with her, by stumbling over my words when I spoke with her, by tripping over my own feet at the front of the classroom accidentally, and by being complimented by Mr. Cope for having my history homework completed and reading ahead in English.

None of that worked.

I also tried inane compliments. "You have great hair." I told her. "I wish I had your hair."

She did have great hair. Long, black, straight, and silky-looking hair that reached all the way to her waist and, to me, her incredible hips. I knew though that it was far safer to compliment her hair than her hips.

"Silly! You don't want hair this long! It's so much work!" And then she fanned her hair out over my desk for a moment before expertly gathering it up to one side of her head and pulling it in front of her and away from me.

I didn't tell her how much I appreciated the work she put into her hair or how much I wanted to run my hands through it. That seemed almost as dangerous as complimenting her hips. But I think she gathered as much, because she said, "Thanks for the compliment, but if you touch my hair and my brother finds out, he'll kill you. He's super protective of me."

I didn't ask how he'd find out. I knew. She'd tell him. "David Garlick had the audacity to touch my hair! And he's fascinated by my hips!" She'd tell him that for the pleasure of watching her brother kill me. So I didn't touch her hair. But having it all there in front of me, five days a week, was a kind of exquisite torture for twelve-year-old me, from September to April.

And then in April I brought my homemade, personal electric fan to school. I'd constructed a small box to hold two D batteries, glued the eighty-five-cent motor into place at one end of the box, with a red plastic balsa wood glider propeller glued onto the motor. By connecting the wires coming from the motor to both ends of the batteries, the propeller would spin. I would point it at myself and be far cooler than anyone else in the class. In fact, I thought, having such a device on my desk would make me the coolest kid in the class.

Everyone would be jealous of me and impressed by my technological know-how. Perhaps even Bethany Langer would be impressed and fall in love with me.

That's not, as you've probably guessed, how things turned out.

The fan worked at keeping me cool and earned the notice and admiration of Mr. Cope. "Pretty neat, Dave! You made that yourself?"

A couple of the boys in class were also intrigued. "Where'd you get the motor?" "How'd you know that it was gonna work?"

Bethany, though, was less than impressed. When I initially hooked it up in class it was pointed at her, and it blew her fascinating and exquisite hair out of its usual state of perfection.

"Don't point that thing at me again, okay? Geez!"

For the rest of the morning, I had to be satisfied with the compliment from Mr. Cope and the couple of boys who thought it was kind of neat. At least, I thought to myself, I'm not sweating like a pig and smelling up the place with my sweaty armpits which was a new and unwelcome part of adolescence, and another reason, I thought, Bethany Langer would never fall in love with me.

However, things took a terrible turn later that morning. Just before lunch, Bethany fanned her hair out over my desk which was usually something I really enjoyed. But this time, her fascinating and exquisite hair got caught up in the propeller of my fan, which quickly wound itself up, over and over, from her hair's end, which again, reached all the way to her hips, to her scalp, while she screamed, "TURNITOFFTURNITOFFTURNITOFF!"

As quickly as I could, I disconnected the batteries, but by then, my personal electric fan looked as though it had become one with Miss Bethany Langer.

"Idiot! Garlick, you're an idiot! Now I'm going to have to go home and cut off all my hair! I'm going to be bald and it's all your fault! Idiot! My brother is going to kill you!"

And then Bethany ran out of the classroom crying. The bell rang, and we all went home to lunch.

I went home to wait for death.

I told my mother what had happened, leaving out the fact of my unrequited love for Bethany Langer and her incredible hips.

"Do you know where she lives? We can call her and apologize."

"She's still going to be bald, and her brother is still going to kill me."

"It can't be *that* bad, can it?" she asked.

"I don't know *any* bald girls, do you?"

There weren't *any* Langers in the phone book though, so it wasn't possible to call to apologize, anyway.

Although I spent much of lunch looking out the window for him, Death didn't come by at lunch. But Bethany didn't return to school after lunch either. Mr. Cope told me that he didn't think what had happened was my fault, but it was cold comfort to me. At least I'll go to my death knowing that Mr. Cope didn't hold me responsible, I thought.

After school, I walked home by myself, waiting for Bethany's brother to jump out from behind a tree or pull up on a motorcycle and, after running me over, beat me to death with a stick. I realized that I had no idea what Bethany's brother looked like, but that whoever came up to me with murder in his eyes would probably be him.

Just before supper, a meal I thought might be my last, there was a knock on the front door. I went to answer it, walking as though I was Jimmy Cagney walking towards the electric chair at the end of a movie.

I opened the door to find Roland Markham, the young man who'd become my hero in 1968 by turning his desk into a crystal radio.

"Are you David Garlick?"

"Yes, sir." I called him sir, even though he was my brother's age and in my brother's classes at high school. He was six years older than I was, but he was the same size as every other kid in my Grade 7 class. His voice sounded like a cross between sandpaper on metal and the squeak of a mouse. He had the same impressive case of adolescent acne I was worried about developing, and it didn't look as though he'd washed his hair that month.

"Here's your fan back. It still works. There's a couple of Beth's hairs wrapped around the motor spinny thing though. It's pretty cool! Did you get the motor at Janisse's?"

"Yes, thanks! How do you know Bethany?" I asked.

"You mean Beth? She's my sister. Well, half sister. Her mom married my dad last year."

So this was the brother sent to kill me.

"I'm awfully sorry about Bethany's hair. Did she have to cut it all off?"

"Nah! Once she calmed down, we unwound things pretty easily."

"So you're not going to kill me?

"*Kill* you? Where'd you get a stupid idea like that? I just didn't want my idiot sister to throw your fan away!"

"Still, please tell Bethany I'm sorry, okay? I don't want her hating me because of this."

"I don't know if relaying an apology will help, but I'm happy to tell her. Have a good evening, okay?" And with that, he left.

I'm pretty sure that Bethany hated me for a good long time. She didn't speak to me, or call me silly, or laugh her laugh of many small bells at anything I said for a very long time. She also started to tie her hair in a long single braid, which was far less fascinating to me, though she still had great hips.

I apologized profusely and wrote her the very best "I'm sorry for being an idiot" letter I could, but I'm pretty certain she continued to hate me, at least for the rest of the month. By the end of the school year though, things had gotten back to almost normal between us, and I'd begun to notice that Michele Luciani and Sheila Mitchell were at least as attractive to me as Bethany had been.

But I never brought the fan to school again.

The Short but Profitable Career of Jeremy Blendick, Professional Insulter

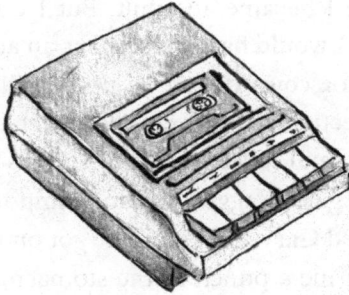

There are several conversations I wish I'd had as a teenager, told certain people how I felt about them, asked others questions that I had about them. Writing these stories has, in a way, given me that opportunity. The stories "improve" actual conversations sometimes. They change the words I used and make me sound funnier or more intelligent or more sensitive than I was.

This is hard for me to admit to you, gentle reader. I was not always the person I am now. The only thing that allows me to admit this, is that none of us are. We all grow. We all change. We are all in constant metamorphosis. Most of us get better.

When I was in high school, I had a number of friends who were gay. Did I know they were gay? Not really. Oh, I was pretty sure, but we never spoke about it. They never told me. I never asked. If we had talked about it, I'm pretty sure we would have remained friends. I'm pretty sure I wouldn't have "outed" them to anybody else.

But here's the thing, because it didn't happen, I don't know any of that either. I like to think I would have acted honourably, the way I do now, the way I have for the decades since I became an adult. But I don't know that that's the way I would have behaved as an adolescent.

I was often a coward. I stood up to bullies rarely, and usually, ineffectually. For example, when Gary Shipton (not his real name) called one of my friends who I thought probably was gay, a faggot, I didn't jump to his defence. Instead, I asked Gary what mark he got on the day's math test. It earned me a punch in the stomach, and a kick in the ass, and it diverted attention away from my friend, but it was really pretty cowardly.

If I had jumped to his defence, and asked Gary why he thought it was any business of his, or anyone else's for that matter, maybe my friend would have known I was an ally and that he could depend on me as a friend.

And maybe I would have known it too.

Gary Shipton had no business being in high school. For starters, he didn't *look* like a high school kid. He had a full beard and moustache at thirteen years of age. He was six foot one, and he told us he weighed 240 pounds. I, at 118 pounds, had no way of verifying it, but I thought he was closer to a ton. I don't know that he passed a single class in high school except for phys ed.

In our phys ed changing room, he had the demeanour of a professional wrestler. Each day, in Grade 9, he would "sneak up" on Daniel Parent, pick him up over his head, and place him on the shelf above the hooks we hung our clothes on. Sometimes Daniel was fully clothed, sometimes he was butt naked. Sometimes he was wet from the shower, sometimes he was dry, having just walked into the changing room.

I put "sneak up" in quotes because there was no actual sneaking up. Shipton would begin flexing his muscles and stomping around the room. Some kids would laugh. Daniel would roll his eyes and look at me dejectedly, or he'd look just as dejectedly at any one of six or seven other kids, who like Daniel, did not see any humour in this.

And then Shipton would pick Daniel up, hold him horizontally over his head, and place him on the shelf where we placed our shoes and gym bags. Daniel was as different from Shipton as any two kids in Grade 9 could be. Daniel weighed, maybe, eighty-five pounds, had yet to sprout any of the body hair that the rest of us were beginning to deal with, and his voice had yet to change.

"Why don't you tell Carter?" we asked in the cafeteria after gym. "We" being the seven or eight kids in the class who found no humour in Shipton's daily antics. Mr. Carter, our phys ed teacher, was a decent guy, and we didn't think he'd put up with what Shipton was doing if he knew about it.

"Why do you think?" Daniel exclaimed in his pre-adolescent, feminine-sounding voice. "If I, or any of you for that matter, complain to the teacher, Shipton might not set me down so gently! He might throw me against the wall! He might *accidentally* drop me from a great height! Do you think he cares if he gets kicked out of school? It'd just speed up his career towards joining a street gang or becoming a World Wide Professional Wrestler!"

"This week's feature bout . . . Dazzling Danny takes on the One-Boy Freak Show! Sandwich Town's very own Shit Stain! Gary 'the Snake' Shipton!" Jeremy Blendick said all this, somehow whispering, yet somehow doing an excellent impression of the voice of Sam Simpkins, the announcer for World Wide Professional Wrestling. Even if you didn't watch WWPW on Saturday afternoons, you knew Sam Simpkins's voice from the TV and radio commercials.

We laughed uproariously at this. Jim Parkins almost choked to death on his daily cheese sandwich, laughing all the while.

"Stop it, Jeremy!" I said. "You'll make my milk come out my nose again." Back in September, Jeremy *had* made my milk come out of my nose.

"Gary the Skunk Shipton! He beats his opponents with the power of his smell! Free nose plugs with every ticket purchased."

We laughed at this too but not as hard as we had at "Sandwich Town's Shit Stain." I'd never heard those words put together, but it made me see the use and purpose of

Mrs. Lanktree's lessons on alliteration. Plus, we were all thirteen- or fourteen-year-old boys.

"Man, I'd love to see you say that kind of stuff to Shipton! Watch his big pig face sour up. D'you think it'd make him stop picking up Danny?" Donald Larriviere asked.

"I dunno. I *do* think it'd make him punch Jeremy in the face though," I said.

"Yeah. You guys would have to agree to pay for my medical bills, and maybe my funeral." Jeremy finished the conversation off for the day.

As much as we'd have liked to see Shipton taken down a peg, none of us wanted Jeremy to get beaten up for it.

The next day, just as Shipton was winding himself up to pick Daniel up, Jim Parkins said, "Hey, Gary? Why not give it a rest for today? Or maybe the rest of the week? Heck, just stop, okay? Even the best jokes get stale if you keep telling them, and you've told this one, what, a hundred times?"

Over the years, I've thought of this little speech a lot. There was nothing insulting about it. Jim didn't even imply that picking up Daniel wasn't funny. He just pointed out that even the best jokes don't benefit from being told again and again. The only thing *wrong* in Shipton's eyes could have been that Jim had been brave enough to say it in front of all of us. Jim hadn't even stood up to say it. He said it while seated and tying his running shoes, as casually as he could.

"Waddya want me to do instead? Rearrange your face for you?"

"No. I like it pretty much the way it is, thanks."

We were all impressed by how cool Jim remained through all this.

Then Daniel said, in his quiet, effeminate voice, "Leave him alone, Shipton. If it makes you feel better, you can keep picking me up and placing me on the shelf."

Just then though, Mr. Carter stuck his head in the door and said, "One minute, boys! Time to get yourselves into the gym!"

Shipton finished the discussion off by saying, "Tell you what, ladies. Tomorrow, I won't pick Miss Shrimp up and place her on the shelf. Maybe I'll rearrange Parkins's face for him. Maybe I'll do something else. Maybe it'll be any one of youse."

So the conversation at lunch that day was not as humourous. We all commended Jim and Daniel for their bravery, but none of us were laughing that day. Jeremy Blendick was unusually quiet. But just before the bell rang to end lunch, he said, "Tell you guys what. You won't need to pay for my funeral, or my medical bills. Any one of us could be the Shit Stain's focus tomorrow. Any one of us could get our features rearranged. If each of you promise to buy me one bowl of chili a week," he looked around at us, "so that means, since there are seven of you, I get one bowl of chili each week for almost two months, if you guys do that, I'll make myself his focus tomorrow. Deal?"

We quickly agreed. I like to think that we agreed not out of fear, and not really thinking Jeremy would get his features rearranged, but because we all wanted to see and hear what Jeremy would say, what he thought would be *worth* maybe getting punched in the face and becoming the daily focus of the biggest bully we'd ever known. Whatever each of our reasons were, we all agreed to buy Jeremy a bowl of chili, which was one of the best foods our cafeteria served.

"Anticipation" isn't really the best word for what we felt the next morning. None of us wanted anyone to get hurt. All of us, at least all of us in the lunch group, wanted Daniel to be left alone. All of us wanted Gary Shipton to stop being such a bully.

Jeremy arrived at the changing room before the rest of us and was sitting on the bench already changed and ready for gym class. Shipton was the last to arrive that morning, making an entrance. He puffed his chest out and announced, "Well, boys and girls! Who's it gonna be today? Who's gonna be my *girl*friend today? You, Parkins? You, Garlick? I don't think I can lift either one of you over my head. I'll probably drop you. Uh'course it'd be by accident, and I'd try to break your fall with my knee."

Our attention was drawn away from Gary Shipton by Jeremy Blendick. "No, Shit Stain. I think you should try to pick me up instead."

Jeremy's voice sounded different than usual, kind of like Edward G. Robinson in any one of the mobster movies I'd seen him. I thought that if it was me, my voice would sound far more quavering and higher pitched.

"What did you call me?" Shipton had balled his hands into fists.

"I called you Shit Stain, see?" Now it sounded just like Edward G. Robinson. "Gary Shipton. You, sir, are the skid mark on the BVDs of mankind. Gary Shit-ton, a regular Turd Sw—"

Mr. Carter interrupted Jeremy by sticking his head into the room and saying, "Class time, boys! Let's get out there!"

"You're dead after class, Blendick!" Gary's hands were balled even tighter, and his face had gone red.

"Why me?" Jeremy said, in the same quavering and high-pitched voice I thought I would have had.

But then, in Edward G. Robinson's voice he added, "I don't think so, Mr. Shit-ton. Hey, Jimmy? Tell Mr. Carter that Blendick'll be out in a minute, okay? He's gotta make himself pretty for the Shit Stain."

We all left Jeremy alone in the change room, and true to his word, he joined us after only a couple minutes.

"Sorry, Mr. Carter. I was indisposed."

I have no memories of the activities we did that day. I do remember Shipton making eye contact with Jeremy several times and mouthing, "You, me" and then warming his knuckles, his right hand punching into his left.

"You're not my type, Gary," was Jeremy's response.

At the end of class, Jeremy raced into the changing room, seemingly eager for his encounter with destiny. Shipton entered the change room, ready to *really* rearrange Jeremy's features.

"If you don't like the sight of blood, you'd better beat it," Shipton told us.

Jeremy smiled and in his very best Edward G. Robinson voice he said, "I'd do what the man says, see? You don't want to see what I'm gonna do to him, either."

We could not believe what we were hearing, but we didn't want to be in the same small area as these two guys tried to rearrange each other's faces. So we all picked up our gym bags and went into the hall.

We listened at the door but heard nothing at first—maybe something like a plastic toy breaking, a bit of laughter, but no shouting or screaming. Just quiet.

Two or three minutes later, Gary Shipton came out, clearly upset, but his features had not been rearranged. In fact, it looked almost as though he was about to cry.

From inside the room, we heard Jeremy say, "Remember our conversation, Mr. Shipton. I'm a man of my word. Do not test me. You'll regret it."

We filed into the changing room. Jeremy sat on the bench where he'd been when we left him. His features hadn't been rearranged either. He'd buttoned his shirt and was holding a broken reel-to-reel audiotape, a jumble of tape in his hands and a smile on his face.

"What happened?" we all asked at the same time.

Tossing the jumble of tape into the waste bucket, Jeremy said, "Someone owes me a bowl of chili. Let's go to the caf and I'll explain."

Usually, we each went to our lockers to drop off our gym bags, but we were all so eager to hear that we went to the cafeteria holding our gym bags. I bought Jeremy his first bowl of chili.

"Here's what happened, see?" said Jeremy 'Edward G. Robinson' Blendick. "None of you mugs saw that I'd brought my tape recorder into the changing room this morning before school, or that I'd turned it on just before

Shipton came in. So I recorded the whole conversation this morning. Him threatening us. Him calling us ladies. Him saying he'd pick one of us to be his next girlfriend. Edward G. Robinson calling him everything I called him. I just wish I'd had the chance to call him more. I had some really good names thought up that I can't use now." His voice slowly reverted to the normal voice of Jeremy Blendick as he explained all of this.

"I reminded him that my older brother is in charge of morning announcements and the tape would 'accidentally' get played if any of us got hurt or if Daniel ever got picked up again. He probably wouldn't get in too much trouble with the principal, but it would make him the laughingstock of the school and make it really hard to find a date for the prom. My brother would apologize to the principal for playing it and tell him the tape was labelled *The Beatles, 1968*. So anyway, Gary yanked the tape out of my hand and stomped on it, laughing as he did it."

"Yeah. I think we heard that," said Jim Parkins.

"Then I told him that that wasn't the tape. That someone else in class had the tape. Look in your gym bags."

We each had a cassette tape in our bags. Each was labelled *The Beatles, 1968*.

"Here's the deal. I promised Shipton that if he left us *all* alone, the tape would never see the light of day. I also promised him that none of us would ever call him any of the things I called him today, apt though they may be. So, in addition to the chili, I need your *words* you'll never call him anything bad. Okay? He stops bullying us, and we don't bully him. I gave him my *word*. Fair?"

Gary Shipton never bothered any of us again. Jeremy got a free bowl of chili every week for the rest of our high school careers.

Most of us got a free tape of the Beatles' White Album that day. Jeremy knew I already had a copy of the White Album, so he gave me a different tape instead. I destroyed it after I finished writing this story.

Four Fine Teachers

Some of the people who read my first book were disappointed by things I left out. Kids who'd gone to school with me were upset that I barely mentioned the band and didn't even mention the many championship teams I hadn't played on. Some were disappointed that I hadn't talked about their favourite teacher. The thing was, though, that being a favourite teacher did not mean that they were connected to an actual story.

I added it up. In my first book I mention almost thirty teachers by their real names. In every case they were, or are, fine teachers. If I did not use a teacher's real name, it didn't *necessarily* mean that they weren't fine. Maybe I couldn't locate them to ask their permission to put them in a book. Maybe I'd fictionalized them to the point I didn't think it fair to use their real name. Or, maybe, they just weren't a fine teacher.

The four teachers in this section were or are, in my opinion, each the finest kind. They weren't mentioned in my first book. Although they aren't associated with any actual stories, I think they deserve a place here. They appear in the order I encountered them: from Mr. Renaud in Grade 9 to Don Learn, as a principal, only a few years ago.

Paul A. Renaud

I don't know what the "A" stood for. When asked, he would always give a different answer. The names he chose would always make us, a group of thirteen- and fourteen-year-olds, laugh and laugh. I prefer to think it stood for "Abercrombie," because his mock indignation that followed the laughter seemed almost genuine in that case.

Since I joined Facebook, I've discovered that Mr. Renaud was not universally loved as a teacher, but I loved him. To me, he was a fantastic teacher of math, who made the subject both interesting and fun. He taught me how to use a compass and protractor correctly. Every day, he told us a joke. And he did an excellent job of keeping my "math ego" in check. I was pretty good at thirteen. And while, in most respects, my ego was not something that ever required being placed in check, it was in certain subjects, math among them. Mr. Renaud did it in such a way that I laughed harder than anyone else in class.

Once, for example, when I'd asked a particularly silly question, (and most teachers, if they're being honest, will disagree with you when you say there's no such thing as a silly question): "Ahhh . . . Mr. Garlick . . . Class?" he said, looking around the room. "You may not know this, but David was born as one of a pair of twins. It's true! A boy and an idiot. Sadly, the boy died . . ."

Roy DelCol

In a positive sense, more than any other person, Roy is the reason I became a teacher of history. I had some excellent teachers, both in high school and university, but professors taught me nothing about teaching. With respect to history, that was Roy DelCol.

Some of this may not sound significant, or even appropriate, but you didn't know me in high school. Roy was, and is, bright, bright, bright; one of the smartest men with respect to history I'd ever met and a fine teacher. He was also in the Canadian Navy, the commanding officer of the HMCS Hunter, and a stickler for discipline. He impressed on me the importance of exactness of language in history and the correct use of footnotes and bibliography. He was the first teacher who told us that he would stop marking a paper if there were more than three spelling mistakes on a page and if the margins weren't exactly one and a half inches on the left and an inch on the top, bottom, and right. I made sure they were. I also did my best to ensure that there were zero spelling mistakes on each page.

And Roy was hilarious.

You have to understand, what follows happened every time there was a test. If you remember high school tests, you remember that they could be very stressful, particularly if you really liked the teacher and didn't want to disappoint them. During every test, he'd stand at his podium for the entire class. He wasn't at attention or anything. He would be reading or marking. He wouldn't move though, and soon we'd forget that he was there, which I think was the point. As we were writing, some of us doing well, but some of us stressed and, maybe, not doing well, we'd hear a quiet droning kind of noise. "Errrrrrrr." At first, none of us could identify the source, and we weren't *really* certain we were hearing it at all. Then it got louder, and we'd see it was coming from Roy DelCol. Whereas at the start of the test, he'd been paying us little attention, now he was looking right at us. His hands gripping the top of the podium, the droning getting louder and louder.

It became clear to the class that he was pretending to fly a plane. A fighter plane. A World War I fighter plane. And then—

"Ack-ack-ack-ack." He was firing the plane's machine guns, this time aimed right at me. "Ack-ack-ack-ack. Garlick! Garlick! You're going down in flames!"

The class would laugh, any tension we'd been feeling, broken. I laughed harder than anyone. Partly because it was just so funny, but partly because I knew it meant that Roy somehow *knew* I was doing well.

The next day, before Roy would have had the chance to get the tests marked, someone would always ask how they'd done. Someone had to ask, because it was expected, and necessary for the joke, and the show.

He'd hold up one hand, making the universal symbol for zero, and then he'd sing to the person who'd asked, in a very nice tenor voice, "Shine on, shine on, harvest moon!"

Love that man.

Bob Bellaire

I was never a very good vice-principal. That's not me being humble when I write that; it's just me being honest. I was never a very good vice-principal.

I *tried* to be good, but I never got the hang of being a disciplinarian. I'd never needed to be, as a teacher. I guess I thought I wouldn't need to be as a VP either, but it didn't turn out that way.

I can't count the number of times I said to people, "I don't get it. I was a *good* teacher, a *really* good teacher. You know, I could get 90 percent of a Grade 12 history class to understand Turner's Frontier Thesis the first time I taught it to them!" (You don't need to understand the Turner Thesis, or even to have heard of it to understand the frustration in this. You just need to know that it's a really complex idea.) "And the 10 percent who didn't get it right away? They got it the next day. Now as VP, I can't teach *one* kid, one-on-one, to understand that he can't stick a pen in someone's ear."

I was just never very good.

Bob Bellaire heard me talking like this in the staff room, a place I hardly ever got to during lunch anymore. Now Bob was not a *good* teacher. Bob was a *great* teacher, one of the very best I ever knew. Bob was the assistant head of science, in the last year of his career. He was a bear of a man, six foot two or three. Full head of white hair. An almost permanent smile. Bob was beloved by the kids and the teachers, me included.

"Come with me," he said.

We got up and left the staff room.

"Where are we going?" I asked.

"We're just going for a walk," he answered. "No place in particular. I was worried that people would think they were helping by agreeing with you, and I didn't want to argue with anyone today. Here's the thing, Dave. You *are* doing a good job. You *are,* because you care about the kids. And that's what *these* kids need. They need someone like you on their side."

"Well, thanks, but—"

"There's no 'but.' You are doing a good job and it's an important job. These kids . . ." He stopped in the hall and waved his arms indicating that he was talking about everybody. "These kids *need* someone like you in their corner. Some schools don't even need a vice-principal. Kennedy *Collegiate* doesn't. Kennedy just needs a picture of someone in a suit with a little brass plaque underneath saying 'Vice-Principal.' On the first day of school, the teachers take all their Grade 9 kids past the picture and say that if they get into any trouble—do anything stupid— they'll have to meet *him*! That's all they need. The kids here wouldn't respond to that, and it wouldn't scare them. Our kids don't *need* to be scared. They need someone they can respect and someone they know cares about them. That's you!"

We walked a little further, and then he tousled my hair, like he would a student—the way my father did when I was a kid, the way Bob almost certainly did with *his* children. "So listen: I don't ever want to hear you saying that you're not doing a good job again, okay?"

Don Learn

I never had the opportunity to work with Mr. Learn and I was never in one of his classes, but that doesn't mean I haven't learned from him, that he hasn't taught me.

Don was an elementary school principal, but by the time I got to know him, he'd retired from that and was a wizard with a camera. He'd been that kind of wizard for a pretty long time, but I hadn't known that. I remember him coming up to me in my last year at Walkerville, after we'd finished staging *To Kill a Mockingbird*.

"Here. I took some black and white pictures of the performance. I thought *Mockingbird* was better served by black and white."

He passed me over a number of folios, a book, and a USB stick.

"I made copies for each of the actors and one for you. I thought your introduction to the play was excellent, and it *needed* to be said, to place the play in perspective. I hope you don't mind, but I took a couple pictures of you too. The pictures are all yours. Do with them what you want."

A couple years earlier, he showed up at Forster. "Here. I know that you're involved with the Duff-Baby Mansion. I stopped by a couple weeks ago and took some pictures of the house in the snow." He then went on to tell me the techniques that he'd used, the time of day, the ratio of sun to cloud, the speed of the aperture, that kind of thing. I listened—well, tried to listen—but I was so taken with the pictures, printed in poster sized format, along with the more regular sized 4" x 6" ones, that I'm afraid I didn't *really* hear what he was saying. "The pictures are all yours. Do with them what you want."

When we held the ceremony to open the mansion to the public, he showed up, parked himself and his walker against a walnut tree, and took photos throughout the event. Later: "The pictures are all yours. Do with them what you want."

Don Learn is, and always has been, generous—no, self-less—with his talents.

We began an email relationship. Kind of a "pen pal" thing. But I'll also stop by his home every once in a while, and he's been over here with his wife Diana too. It turns out that he's also a wizard with language too. Listen to this:

"Words are the elixir of living.

"Just because you have ailments that limit, don't stop living while the sheets are still warm.

"Your writing has a stamp that is rich in its candour and rooted in the historical garden. In the context of reading your work, the pen of Will Rogers pops off the page."

Or

". . . but back to the books. Your tool of choice is not the harrow, where you tickle the surface, but the plough where you dig deep and turn the soil for the richness beneath. I am one of the many who thank you for keeping the story alive."

I mean, yes, I know that the compliments are hyperbolic, but I get to read them and read them again, as I know you will now. And these are just *emails*! Written, seemingly, as easily as a shopping list.

And all I ever have to do to get one of those things is ask how he's doing.

Like Roy DelCol, I love that man.

Part Two:
David as Teacher

The Beginning of Teachers' College: *This* Is Higher Education?

I hesitate to write this story for a couple reasons. First, it presents an odd view of teachers' college, and secondly, because it is so odd, people might think that it's not true. It's absolutely true. Teachers' college was not all like this. This is just the way it started for me.

The first time I was homesick was when I went to teachers' college in Kingston. I was all by myself, 600 or so kilometres from home, with no one to talk to. I've since found that is the only thing that can make me homesick: being alone, with no one to talk to.

My parents helped me move to Kingston in early June. This was my idea. Arriving so early, I'd be able to get a good handle on the city, know where everything was, the grocery store, the bus stops, my school—everything. I would get used to cooking for myself and doing all my own laundry. It was a pretty smart idea, I thought.

It was also wrong.

Oh sure, I found out how long it would take to walk to school each morning and where to lock my bike on the days I took my bike. I became adept at making steak and rice dinner, a master of the grilled cheese sandwich and the clean out the fridge omelette. But I was alone. I had no friends, and really, no way to make any for more than two months. While I wasn't exactly poor, I did not have extra money for long-distance phone calls home. Letters took a few days to get to Windsor, and even if my friends responded right away, it took another few days for a letter to get back to me.

I read. I walked. I rode my bike. I listened to the radio.

I was lonely and homesick.

For two long months, I crossed the days off my calendar to mark when school would start, and I'd get to meet people, people who wanted to be teachers like me.

Then, finally, the day arrived. I went to Duncan MacArthur Hall to pick up my schedule and meet a few people, on the Friday before school was scheduled to start, which was on the Tuesday after Labour Day.

As I compared schedules with all my new-found potential friends, I saw that many of them, the majority I spoke with, had a short-term class valued at a half credit. It would be completed within a month, and it started the next day, on a *Saturday*. It was called Effective Speech in the Classroom.

I didn't have this class on my schedule. Me being me, I *knew* that if I didn't take it, come the end of the school year, someone at the university would tell me that I couldn't graduate. After all, how could someone become a teacher without passing Effective Speech in the Classroom?

So, I sought out my counsellor, whose name was on my schedule and who was also my professor of history. I knocked quietly on his office door, which was answered by a very friendly man who invited me in and asked me to take a seat. I explained my issue and posed my question to him: "Do I need this class? If I don't take it this weekend, will I still be able to graduate come May?"

He didn't really answer right away but asked me a related question. "So, if you're not taking this Effective Speech class, does that mean you've got nothing to do this weekend?"

I answered truthfully. "Yes. I guess I don't. I'm really looking forward to your class, though."

"Well then. I guess you might as well just start things a little early! Here's the syllabus. Here are the first few readings you'll need to take care of, and here's your first assignment. Oh, and don't worry about that Effective Speech thing. It's not required."

So I went home feeling much better about things. I didn't need to worry about Effective Speech in the Classroom. School would start in three days. I'd met my history prof, who seemed a decent sort, and I actually had some work to do!

I forget what the readings were, and the assignment. I remember that they were all done by Saturday afternoon, and that if teachers' college was going to be like this, it was going to be a snap.

Two and a half days later, I was sitting in my first class, my history class, looking at the class of thirty or so other people who also were going to be history teachers. Just like me! Thirty potential friends! My loneliness was almost at an end.

Then my professor walked in. The *very* first thing he did was walk over to me, put his hands on my shoulders, and say, "Class? I'd like you to meet David Garlick. He came to my office on Friday to ask for extra work. Now, some of you might call that sucking up, but it's what you're going to have to do if you want to get by in this course."

I watched thirty pairs of eyes immediately assess David Garlick as a suck-up, who it would be best to avoid. I couldn't very well disagree with my *professor,* one of the people who was guarding the door between me and my chosen career.

I'd be lonely for a little bit longer.

Later that week I went to a class called the Sociology of Deviant Behaviour. I thought it would be both interesting and useful. The first class dealt with witchcraft, which I thought was interesting, maybe not really useful, but interesting and deviant, I guess. It was a twelve-week class. Once a week. Full credit. Every Thursday.

There was no homework that I remember.

The following Thursday, the professor dealt with witchcraft again. Not so interesting this time. And given all the deviant behaviours we could be dealing with, well, not really very useful.

The third Thursday, he brought in an ex-witch to talk with us. A guest speaker.

She talked about the last time she'd called herself a witch. She told us she'd drawn a pentagram on her apartment floor, with candles and whatever, and summoned whoever witches were supposed to summon, and then she pounded on the professor's desk, shouting, "And the devil? The *devil*? He was a-rappin' on my window!"

I bit my cheek to keep from laughing. My friend, for by now I had made friends, put up his hand and asked, "May I ask what drugs you were using at this time?"

I thought it incredibly, I don't know, rude? Until she began to list the drugs she'd had in her system that evening. I learned a little bit that day about the relationship between drugs and deviant behaviour, but to be honest, it wasn't something I didn't already know. And now the class, for which we weren't given a syllabus, was a quarter finished, and we'd only talked about witches and a little bit about drugs because of my friend's irreverence, which I guess is a better descriptor than rude.

The following Thursday turned out to be a very important day in my life and career. We were a month into the school year. I was about to learn that I was no longer the same person who'd asked his counsellor about Effective Speech in the Classroom, the person who had quietly accepted it when he was falsely accused of being a suck-up.

The professor walked in and said something about how interesting the guest speaker had been and how he thought it best to continue the conversation about witchcraft.

I put up my hand. The professor sat on the front of his desk, pointed at me, and said, "Yes, young man?"

"Sir? Including this year, I've been in education for only eighteen years. But in all that time, I've never encountered even a single witch." There were twenty students in this class. I did some quick math in my head. "If everyone here has only my number of year's experience in education there are 360 combined years represented here. May I ask, in all that time, how many of you have encountered even *one* witch?"

A student put up his hand and responded to me, "There was a girl in Grade 5 who *said* she was a witch and could recite the alphabet backwards."

"Yes, and as students in Grade 5, how did you deal with that?"

"Well, we kind of ignored it. It wasn't really important."

"Sir? With all due respect, I assume that most students took this class, like I did, thinking it would be of some use to us as teachers. So, when you choose to deal with something other than witchcraft, I'll be back."

And then I got up and left the room, thinking, as I left, What the hell am I doing? I am never going to graduate if I lose this credit. Who is this guy I've become? Maybe I can apologize at the end of the day. Maybe he'll let me back in next week . . . But I kept walking. I opened the door and left the room.

I was followed by, I think, seven or eight other students, and then the professor, who rushed out and stopped *us*, not just me. "Wait, wait. Okay. No more witchcraft. Please. Come back in."

Forty years later, I have no other memories of this class. It's completely gone. It was, in almost all respects, completely valueless. I encountered deviant behaviours in almost every month of my career and became pretty adept at working with them, but not because of this course or anything that professor tried to teach us.

But on that day, a third of the way through the course, it taught me what it was, and how it felt to be a leader, and how much teachers' college, and this career, would change me.

The Overdose

Note: Please don't worry. As you've probably noted by now, this book is intended, in the main, to be funny. Despite the title of this story, no one gets rushed to the hospital. No one dies. No one even does anything illegal.

During my first practice teaching session, in Ottawa, I was put in charge of teaching a Grade 13 class. They were all really bright, and good students, but their teacher was concerned that they were too accepting of the information they were given by him. They didn't question him, just writing down everything he said.

"Well, at least it seems they accept you as an expert," I said.

"Yes. But I want them questioning things. I want them to think critically. They're almost finished high school. They need to think for themselves."

So I went home and developed a lesson of lies.

Classes were seventy-five minutes long. I made up a lecture, telling the class that this would be like most of their university experience, which would start in only a few months, so they'd better get accustomed to it. I wrote an outline on the board to help them along and told them they'd have to make their own notes. I'd collect them at the end of class, read them over that night, and give them a mark out of 100.

After a little bit of general grumbling, my associate teacher said, "For as long as he's here, Mr. Garlick is your teacher, so you'd better do what he says." The class settled down for the rest of the period.

The lecture started out reasonably enough. I'd decided to stop delivering my lecture of lies as soon as a student questioned me about any of them. Any student, any lie. I spoke for almost sixty minutes. The kids were madly trying to keep up. I wasn't interrupted, and my associate sat at the back of the class smiling for the hour. I don't remember the topic or anything that I said that day, except for the last statement: "Joshua Lefkowitz was the first bus driver to be able to turn a city bus around inside the Detroit-Windsor Tunnel, in 1947."

One girl put up her hand. "Sir?"

"Good!" I responded. "Asking a question is an excellent way to slow the class down. It allows you to catch up."

"No. I was going to ask you what Joshua Lefkowitz has to do with anything. I mean, why do we need to know about a bus driver?"

"You don't. I made the name up last night."

"What?"

"I made it up. In fact, I made up everything I've been talking about for the last hour. No one interrupted me, so I just kept talking. If anyone had stopped me, or questioned anything I've said, I would have stopped. You've all spent the last hour writing down a bunch of lies."

"But . . ."

"Studying history is not about accepting everything you read or hear. It's about reading and hearing but then asking questions about it. It's about judging whether what you're reading makes any sense, if what you're reading and hearing fits in with everything else you've been reading and hearing about."

"So we've wasted the last hour?"

"Nope. In fact, what you've learned in the last hour may be the most important lesson of the year. Question your teachers. Question what you're reading. Does a writer have a bias you should know about? Does your teacher?"

"Do we still get to hand in our notes to you for marks?"

"Nope. I was lying about that too."

A few of the kids laughed at this. A few were upset. There was some complaining.

"From now on, I want you to start challenging me. Heck, I'd like for you to challenge *all* your teachers! Ask questions like, Who wrote this textbook? Are there any other opinions about this or that? Have people always thought this about that?"

There was still some grumbling. "I've got a cramp in my hand from so much writing." "I wasted five sheets of paper!" But in the main, the class appreciated what had just happened to them and my associate teacher thought the lesson was brilliant.

A few days later, though, my associate told me two things that were unrelated in his mind but caused me great concern. The first was that my professor from teachers' college would be dropping by to assess me, and the second was that he wanted me to debate the class. Me. Against the class.

As a group, the students had responded to my lesson of lies the way I wanted them to. We discussed the bias history writers have, sometimes without knowing it. We discussed primary and secondary source documents and why to be careful with both. They'd become far more wary, at least with me, and would often stop class by asking, "Really?" or "Are you telling us the truth?" or "Why should we believe this?" They were being polite, but it was clear that they didn't want to get caught out again.

Now, I was to debate them, with both my associate and my professor assessing my performance—both gatekeepers between me and my chosen profession.

The topic: Was Lord Durham's report of 1840 racist against French Canadians? I had to argue that there was nothing racist about Lord Durham or his report.

You don't need to know anything about Lord Durham or his report for this story. This isn't a history lesson. All you need to know is that it, and he, were most decidedly racist. He didn't exactly *hate* the French, but he certainly favoured all things English. He was, after all, an English peer during the reign of Queen Victoria, sent to British North America as her representative. It would have been strange if he hadn't been racist.

Now I had to argue that he wasn't, against a class I'd *trained* to question everything I said, a class of students I'd embarrassed just a week before by tricking them to write into their notes that Joshua Lefkowitz had turned his bus around in the Windsor-Detroit Tunnel.

What better way to get back at me than to embarrass me in front of my professor and my associate teacher? I asked myself, How would you respond as a student if you were in the same position? And I knew the answer. I'd tear me apart. I would have joined a study group of classmates to *know* Lord Durham's report, and we would have assembled a list of questions that there was no way I could answer without losing the debate.

Looking back, with the benefit of more than forty years and having been both an associate teacher and a principal, I *know* that it wouldn't have made any difference if I won or lost and that my associate didn't care at all who won. He just wanted to see his students having learned something in the last two weeks.

But in 1982, fresh out of university and, basically, still a kid myself, I *knew* the opposite. If I didn't win, my chances of becoming a teacher would be, well, pretty slim.

So I stayed up late the night before the debate. I studied and studied and wrote and wrote. The young man I was staying with in Ottawa, a friend from the University of Windsor, told me to go to bed, that I'd need to be rested in the morning. I thanked him for his concern and watched him go off to bed before pouring myself another cup of coffee.

I continued to study and write for the rest of the night, getting up from my desk every twenty minutes or so for a fresh cup of coffee. When the pot went empty, I prepared another pot. University students call this "pulling an all-nighter." I'd done this before but usually without so much coffee. Between 11:00 p.m. and six in the morning, I drank five full pots of coffee.

As soon as I got to school that morning, I poured myself another cup of coffee. Coffee was free for teachers, and by the time school started and I walked into class, fresh cup of black coffee in hand, I'd had two more full *pots*. That made seven full pots of coffee.

I didn't know that a person could overdose on caffeine. I don't really even know if that's technically what happened.

Anyway, just before class, I went to the back of the classroom to shake my professor's hand. He told me that my associate had been saying good things about me and that he was looking forward to the class. I thanked both of them, smiled, and returned to the front of the classroom, standing at a lectern. I took attendance as the kids came in.

By the way, in case you're wondering, to this point, the coffee didn't really seem to have had much effect on me. Although I wasn't tired, my hands weren't shaking or anything. My heart wasn't racing. I felt fine.

Class started. I introduced my professor. I introduced the topic for the day. I explained, for my professor's benefit, how the class and the debate would unfold.

I wasn't cocky so much as clinical. We'd flipped a coin the day before and it had been decided that I would start.

As opposed to a written presentation, I'd decided to only list my arguments in point form. With a red pen, I checked each of them off as I finished them. After about three or four minutes, when I reached for the pen, I realized that I couldn't feel my fingers.

This wasn't frightening; it was fascinating. I stopped talking and tapped my right hand with my left hand, and then my left hand with my right hand. Nothing. No feeling at all. Cool!

I looked up, part of me wanting to share this fascinating information. But before I could, I noticed the faces of twenty-seven concerned students, one concerned associate, and one concerned professor. I'd been smiling to myself and tapping my hands for probably only five seconds, but I'd stopped talking and was now tapping and smiling instead.

And then something terrifying *did* happen. My mind went completely blank. I mean, I knew who I was and that I was supposed to be engaging in a debate with a class of Grade 13 students. I knew my professor was there to assess me and that I'd been given the responsibility of proving that a racist wasn't a racist, but when I looked at my notes, I had no memories of creating them. They were in my handwriting, but it was as though somebody else had written them. The notes were good, but they weren't mine.

I looked up at the class again. The same looks of concern were on all their faces.

"So, does anyone have any questions so far?" I asked.

Thankfully, one student took pity on me. At least that's the way I saw it.

"Well, sir, you were talking to us about this . . ." (I use the word "this" even though, in spite of the quotation marks, that's not exactly what she said, because today, as I write this story, I forget what I'd been talking about, and what she said. And, as the twenty-two-year-old student teacher, all those years ago, I'd also forgotten what I'd been talking about.)

I looked down at the notes and saw a check mark next to a point similar to what the student had mentioned and noted that everything above that also had a check mark.

It took about four minutes for my memories of studying and writing to come back to me. I faked it as best I could for those four minutes, working through the points on the notes in front of me, but those four minutes were, for me, the longest four minutes of my life. Those four minutes gave me time to think that I should never drink a cup of coffee again, that maybe I'd be able to explain things to my associate and my professor well enough to give me another chance, that it wouldn't be *too* bad if I had to go back to McDonald's as a manager instead of becoming a teacher, and that not being able to feel my hands should have been more frightening than fascinating to me.

After four minutes though, everything came back, including the feeling in my hands.

I forget if I won the debate. I remember, though, that the kids were kind to me. They had no intention of tearing me apart. None of them. They knew that I'd been assigned the role and also that Durham *was* a racist. It didn't make any difference what I said that day.

They'd done their part of the assignment: read everything they could find about the topic, probably talked to each other about it, listened to their student teacher, and then decided for themselves—exactly what their *real* teacher had wanted of them.

I had played my part exactly as my associate had wanted to. I don't think he'd expected me to drink seven pots of coffee and overdose on caffeine, but he'd expected me to do my best, and I had.

I received an excellent report from him at the end of my session. I received an excellent report from my professor too.

I didn't drink another cup of coffee until I'd graduated from teachers' college, more than six months later.

The Break and Enter

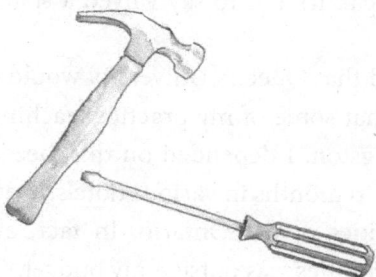

There are a few things you need to know before I can tell you this story: I worked at McDonald's from Grade 11, in 1975, until I finished my undergrad, in 1982. The whole point of my McDonald's career was to save enough money so I wouldn't have to work while in teachers' college.

I was successful in this, but I did not have a lot of extra money. While not poor, I tried to budget between ten and fifteen dollars a week for food. Today, that would be around thirty to forty-five dollars. My favourite gift when I left for teachers' college was a case of canned pasta from my friend Graham White. I did not have a television, I think I saw two movies that year, and my favourite pub was the Queen's Hotel where beer only cost twenty-five cents a glass and my limit was four.

I lived in a basement apartment, and my rent was $225 a month. Again, accounting for inflation, that would be a bit more than $700 a month. My furniture was all the things my parents no longer wanted and had replaced. I walked to school every day and do not remember ever taking the bus anywhere.

I was frugal. It's fair to say I lived a spartan existence that year.

I was told that Queen's University would do its best to make sure that some of my practice teaching would take place in Kingston. I depended on this, because I did not budget for two months in various hotels, even cheap ones, in communities across Ontario. In fact, even travel to those communities was outside my budget.

As things turned out, none of my practice teaching was in Kingston. All of it turned out to be in Ottawa or Oshawa. I was lucky to have a friend I could stay with in Ottawa. By the end of the school year, I also had a friend to stay with in Oshawa.

This story takes place before I had a friend in Oshawa.

I'd never heard of Oshawa's General Vanier Vocational School. Nor, to be honest, had I heard of *any* vocational school. I learned, though, that it was a school for students which concentrated more on hands-on skills than academics, because the students all had learning disabilities. And, to be honest, in addition to never having heard of a vocational school, I didn't really know very much about learning disabilities.

"They'll all have trouble with their academic subjects, Dave," said my English professor. "They'll probably all hate the subjects you teach, English and history, so you'll need to make them fun and non-threatening."

My associate teacher, the teacher who actually taught these kids every day, told me the same thing. He also advised me: "If they ask you a question and you don't know the answer, make one up on the spot. Be quick about it, too. For most of their lives, these kids have suffered because they don't know the correct answers. If they're going to respect you, they need to think you've got the answers." (I've since abandoned this approach, favouring, "I don't know, but I know how we can find out . . ." but I was smart enough then to do as I was told.)

I arrived in Oshawa on the Saturday before I was to start at General Vanier. I forget how I found the hotel that cost twelve dollars a night, but on the Sunday afternoon, my associate, Mr. Eric Liddell, came to pick me up, saying, "You can stay with my wife and me. She says she doesn't mind, and all you have to do is promise that you'll do the same thing for someone else some day." (I have.)

At first, I thought this was great good fortune. Free room and board! But soon, I grew to regret it. Eric meant well, but my daily routine for the first week followed this schedule: wake up at 5:00 a.m.; get taught by Eric for an hour and a half; drive to school for forty-five minutes, being taught the whole way; teach the kids; spend the next hour being told what I'd done wrong; have lunch with Eric while being told what I'd done wrong; teach the kids; teach some more kids; drive home, being told what

I'd done wrong; plan for the next day until supper; eat supper; get taught by Eric and plan for the next day until 8:00 p.m.; watch TV until ten; go to bed; and repeat for Tuesday, Wednesday, and Thursday.

By Friday, I was exhausted, developing the worst head cold of my life and beginning to doubt that teaching was for me. Five days of being told everything I was doing was wrong, plus five days when I *believed* that, had caused me to think that maybe working at McDonald's was more my speed.

The kids I was teaching didn't help. They were out of control the whole time I was there. I put none of the responsibility for this on my associate. It was all my fault. (When I became an associate teacher a few years after this, I always told my student teachers that I was responsible for class behaviour, not them. I also told them that one of the most important things to do was to become a real person to the kids, not just a teacher.)

On the Friday after lunch, I walked into class, and the kids were already out of control again. I looked at my associate, who was sitting at the back of the room, and said, "I'm sorry. You'll have to excuse me for a minute." I went to the bathroom and threw up everything I'd eaten for lunch. I also threw up five days of failure.

I left the bathroom not feeling any better and, maybe, resolving to quit teaching at the end of the day.

But waiting outside the bathroom was a beautiful, young English teacher, Angela de Fazio, leaning against the wall.

"You just threw up in there, didn't you." It wasn't a question. She knew. As low as I felt while I was throwing up, I felt even lower then. But I was honest and nodded. "Yes, yes I did."

She smiled. "Don't worry. I spent my whole first month in there throwing up. It comes with the territory. You'll get better. Come back next week, and we'll get Eric to lighten up, maybe leave you alone for a bit."

I'd like to say things got better after this, and, in a sense, they did. I'd resolved to go home to Kingston for the weekend, a change of plan, but one I felt necessary for my mental and physical well-being. I needed to just get away.

The young and beautiful teacher drove me to the bus station after school and told me to pick up some NeoCitran for the cold and sleep for the weekend. "See you bright and early Monday morning, okay?" she said as she dropped me off.

Graham White called me that evening, "Bad cold, eh? I prescribe at least a couple shots of whatever scotch you've got."

I'd already taken the NeoCitran the beautiful teacher advised me to purchase, so it probably wasn't very smart of me to follow Graham's advice as well, but I did.

I fell into one of the deepest sleeps of my life that night. It was a sleep full of dreams. Dreams that weren't *bad* really, but dreams I've never been able to understand either. The dean of education met with me, for example, asking me about my favourite albums. I'd never met the dean before, and couldn't pick him out of a line-up, but, in the dream, I knew it was him and didn't think it odd at all that he looked just like my father and if he turned his head a certain way, just like Alan Alda from M*A*S*H. (What the heck could that all mean?)

At 3:00 in the morning, I heard a knocking on my apartment door, insistent enough to wake me up. It's important that you understand that I *knew* it was the dean of education who wanted to talk to me about *Sergeant Pepper's Lonely Hearts Club Band*. This made complete sense to me.

"Coming, sir! Maybe not the whole album, but I can't think of a better song than 'A Day in the Life'!"

"Oh shit!" I heard from the other side of the door, followed quickly by someone running up the stairs.

It took me a couple seconds to remember how to unlock the door, but when I did, I was surprised to find that the door jam had been pulled away from the frame of the door, and whoever had been trying to break in was maybe ten seconds from actually getting into my apartment. He'd left behind a hammer and screwdriver, which I have to this day. I figured out that they almost certainly didn't belong to the dean of education.

I have no idea what the police thought of the young man, clearly addle-brained and, at the very least, incredibly drunk. (Slur my voice as you read this next bit) "Sorry you had to come all this way, ossifers. I mean, what would he have taken? My old couch? I drank all the scotch and all I've got in here is my books. I wasn't even supposed to be here this weekend. I've got a cold, you know. Do you think he would've hit me with the hammer?"

My landlady commended me the next morning, for preventing a crime and for repairing the damage myself, which I'd done by employing the tools the sneak thief had left behind.

My cold wasn't completely gone by Monday morning, but I was feeling far better and more myself. The department head of English took me aside before class began to say, "A few of us had a word with Eric. You'll be eating lunch with me this afternoon. You should find him a bit more . . . positive today."

To start the day off, one of the students asked me how my weekend had been. It may have been an attempt to throw me off my schedule, but I was happy to tell the story of how I dealt with my cold, my dreams, the break and enter, and narrowly avoiding being murdered. The class laughed and laughed.

So did I.

I got an excellent report at the end of the teaching session and an apology.

"I'm sorry for being so hard on you, Dave. I was just trying to make you into a teacher of kids with learning disabilities. Once you began class with the story of the break and enter, and you had the class in the palm of your hand, I thought maybe I had."

Outdoor Ed

I never called him "Special Ed." I *did* call him "Outdoor Ed" and for that I won't apologize. He earned that nickname too, and he probably saved Nick's life, so I'm happy to confess that I was one of the people that called Ed Partington, "Outdoor Ed."

I met Ed on the first day of teachers' college. Our Educational Psychology class was playing an icebreaker game, Two Truths and a Lie. We were paired off, and we had to tell our partner two things about ourselves that were true and one thing that was a lie. We were supposed to tell these things so that it was difficult to guess which was which.

My assigned partner was a tall young man. Tall and lanky. Better than six foot two or three. He had long brown hair tied in a ponytail and wore an old Montreal Expos baseball cap. He was good-looking in a wholesome, small-town Ontario baseball player kind of way, complete with chiseled features and cleft chin. Clear blue eyes that you just knew had followed hundreds of fly balls from bat to his centerfielder's glove. He smiled a disarming smile when he shook my hand and said, "My name's Ed Partington. I was named after King Edward of England. Umm . . . My favourite colour is, uhh, blue, and, uhh, I want to teach outdoor education."

"Hi. I'm pleased to meet you, Ed! I'm Dave Garlick. I actually grew up on Partington Avenue, so it won't be hard to remember your name. I bicycled to Kingston from Windsor. I was kicked out of Czechoslovakia at the point of a machine gun and . . . let's see . . ."

"That's too many." Ed looked confused.

"What?"

"That's too many. Okay, your name's not Garlick."

"Yes. Yes, it is." Now I was confused.

"There were only supposed to be three statements total."

"Well, my *name's* not one of them! Your name's Ed Partington, right? You were just introducing yourself."

"I guess . . . So your name *is* Dave Garlick?"

"Yes!" I was starting to feel that I was part of an Abbott and Costello skit.

"But you didn't grow up on Partington Avenue."

"Yes, I did! Look. Those statements didn't count. I *am* Dave Garlick. I *did* live on Partington. And I *was* happy to meet you!"

"Oh! Well, I'm glad we got that straight! Those things are all true! Now you need to come up with a lie. Make it a good one, like me saying I was named after King Edward. I was actually named after my grandfather. He was Ed Partington too. Like my dad."

"Doesn't that mean you were named after your dad?"

"I guess." It seemed as though he'd never considered this, as he held his chin between thumb and forefinger and narrowed his eyes, now deep in thought. He brightened after a couple seconds. "So that was kind of a double lie I guess, eh?"

I think you can see why Ed Partington was given the nickname "Special Ed."

It wasn't kind, and when you consider that we were all going to be teachers, it wasn't the most professional thing for them to say, but I had to admit it seemed apt. Almost daily, in our psychology class, he would say something that had us all shaking our heads. Dr. Carpenter was patient with him and treated all of his questions as though they weren't . . . well . . .

"No, Mr. Partington. 'Id' is not a misspelling of 'it.' It's Greek, and it *means* 'it.'. It's the animal part of your personality."

"Well, why didn't Mr. Freud just say, 'it?' Seems pretty simple to me."

That kind of thing.

Ed Partington was also a student leader in my Outdoor Education class. For me, the class was just several weekends of canoeing, rock climbing, orienteering, and camping. I was never going to actually *be* an outdoor ed teacher. For most of the students in the class, Outdoor Ed was a half-credit experiential learning class that would introduce us to outdoor education. For Ed Partington, and twelve of his colleagues, outdoor education was going to be one of their actual teachable subjects.

And Ed Partington was going to be a *great* outdoor education teacher.

Early in October, the class went rock climbing. I forget the name of the place we went, but it was a sheer-face cliff about fifty feet high. We'd trained indoors, so we all knew how to belay, how to use pitons, and how important it was to pay attention to the person climbing if we were manning the safety rope that they'd attached to the cliff face, always a couple feet above or below them.

Although it *seemed* dangerous, it was really a pretty safe activity.

We each made it up and down the cliff face at least two times that day. All of us except Doris Pestowka. Doris was unashamedly afraid of heights and steadfastly refused to even try. None of us blamed her. None of us expected her to try. She was dressed for the activity but had not left the ground.

"Hey, Doris?" Ed asked. "I get that you're afraid of heights. A lot of people are. But it's not *all* heights, right?"

"What do you mean?" Doris asked.

"Well, I mean, you're not afraid of staircases, right?"

"No . . ."

"See this part right here?" Ed said, pointing to three ascending rocks that looked, now that we focussed on them, like three steps. "Do you think you can climb these three steps?"

"Well, sure. I can do that." She climbed the three steps and then turned around and smiled at us.

"Okay. Good, good, good. Now, some people are afraid when they look up at heights, but you've been here all day and doing a great job of spotting, so I don't think you're one of those people, right?"

"Right," Doris said, looking up.

"It doesn't make you dizzy? Can you reach up and stick a piton in that crevice above you then?"

You've probably guessed that Doris did a fair bit of climbing that afternoon. She froze about twenty-five feet up, but within a minute, Ed was next to her calming her, getting her to look up instead of down, and convinced her to keep climbing. She never made it to the top, but she was actually smiling and singing as we slowly lowered her, by the safety rope, from a height of forty feet.

She hugged us all when she made it to the ground and then kissed Ed on the cheek.

In November, our class went on a canoeing and camping trip over the weekend. It was particularly cold that weekend and thin ice had formed over the streams and small lakes we were on. There were thirty-six of us in three great war canoes, twelve to a canoe. Because it was November, and we left on Friday after school, it was dark before we reached our campground. It wouldn't be fair to say we were miserable as we canoed, but our feet and fingers were all aching from the cold, and a few of us asked more than a few times how much further we had to paddle, and when we'd be stopping. Okay, it *would* be fair to say that we were miserable.

Ed was in the back of our canoe, steering, and he'd been singing something by Crosby, Stills and Nash.

"For the love of God, would you please just shut up!" yelled someone from the canoe behind us.

Loud enough for us all to hear, but somehow not really raising his voice, Ed asked, "Are your feet aching?"

Most, if not all of us grumbled a "Yes."

"Your fingers? They hurt too?"

More grumbled affirmatives.

"Then I'm guessing your cheeks are burning a bit too." Ed was quiet for a few seconds, then he added, "So what?"

I was just beginning to think that maybe Ed was a bit crazy in addition to not being very bright.

"Here's the reality. It's November, and it's Ontario. It's cold. Big deal. Is anyone surprised? The fact that your fingers and toes ache is actually a *good* thing. It tells you that there's blood flowing to your extremities and you're not at risk of frostbite. Complain to me if your fingers and toes *don't* hurt, okay?"

And then, less than a minute later, "See that light ahead? That's our campground. We're there in five minutes."

And we were.

Ed had a fire lit in another five minutes, and soon we were all sitting around it singing the same Crosby, Stills and Nash song he'd been singing.

In January, we went orienteering. We were blindfolded, which probably wasn't necessary, and then, in groups of three, we were dropped off in different sections of the wilderness north of Kingston. We had excellent contour maps, compasses, enough food for the day, and a change of clothes in our backpacks. One of us in each group carried a tent big enough for four people, in case something happened and we were forced to spend the night *not* in a cabin.

When we were dropped off and our blindfolds removed, a student leader pointed at the map and said, "Here's where you need to be this evening. Dinner will be waiting for you, and you'll probably smell it from a kilometre away. See you tonight."

There were no fifty-foot cliff faces, and we'd all been trained how to read maps and to use a compass. The weather was crisp and clear, and though it was January cold, there was no snow forecast. But there was a fresh blanket of the stuff. We all knew how to start a fire and set a camp. There were no dangerous wild animals.

Although it *seemed* pretty safe, it was actually pretty dangerous.

My group of three had no issues at all. We had a great time. We followed the map, knew exactly where we were, found a great place to make camp, and lit a small fire to cook our lunches. We were among the first groups to arrive at the assigned spot and got to help make dinner for the class.

Nick Pappas's group wasn't as lucky. Nick started things off badly by telling the two women he was with, that like most females, they probably didn't know how to read a map and to leave that sort of thing to him. He also told them to *please* be careful and not to wander off, or into a frozen stream or something, because he didn't want to have to rescue them. "It's January, and although it may *seem* really cold," he told them, "the streams rarely freeze over, so you're likely to fall through the ice, like in that story by Jack London, *The Firestarter.*"

Kim Brothers rolled her eyes. "Jack London wrote *To Build a Fire*, doofus. Stephen King wrote *Firestarter*. Geez!"

"Whatever. Just don't fall through the ice, okay?" Nick said, as he broke through the ice to his knees in the fast-running stream he hadn't noticed.

It *was* January cold. And though Nick was at no risk of actually drowning, he was at serious risk of frostbite at the very least and maybe even dying.

Ed Partington had had a bad feeling about Nick and his group, because Nick had not shut up on the bus ride to their drop-off spot. In fact, Nick had demonstrated for four months that he always had a hard time shutting up, thought the world of himself, and thought little of the others in our class. We'd nicknamed *him*, Nick Pompous. When Nick got off the bus, with his blindfold still on, Ed Partington got off as well and hid himself behind a tree.

When Nick fell through the ice, Ed held back for a minute, watching to see what would happen. Nick lumbered to the edge of the creek and fell down on its shore.

"Oh, Jesus," said Kim. "Now one of us has to save *you!*"

"You shouldn't have distracted me! Now I'm soaked!"

"Shut up! Now one of us is supposed to strip off and get into a sleeping bag with you! Let me tell you, Nick Pompous, neither one of us really wants to do that! Knowing you, you'll be telling everyone all about it on Monday morning! We're going to have to flip a coin or something."

Nick laughed at this, but then his teeth started chattering, an ominous sign that he was going into shock. The young woman was right. We were taught that, in just such an eventuality, we were supposed to strip down to our skivvies and get into a sleeping bag with the person. The young woman was also probably correct in assuming Nick would be telling everybody about it on Monday. That's the kind of guy he was. He thought of himself as a "man's man," and "God's gift to the females of our species." He'd earned the nickname he'd been given. It was interesting, though, that none of the women I knew felt he was God's gift to them, and they barely tolerated him.

As the young women were fishing through their pockets for a quarter or a nickel, Ed Partington emerged from behind a tree.

"No worries there, Kim. Don't bother, Mary. I guess I'm about as warm as either of you, and I doubt that Mr. Pappas will want to tell too many people he was in a sleeping bag with me."

That's what happened. Ed got into the sleeping bag with Nick for about a half hour, warmed him up, and then loaned him a change of clothes, the pants being a bit too long for him, and the extra pair of woolen socks just thick enough to account for the slightly bigger, dryer hiking boots Ed supplied.

"Nick? I can't speak for the girls, but as long as I get my clothes back, clean, by Monday or Tuesday, I won't tell anybody about this, okay?"

Kim added, "I won't tell anyone as long as you shut up for the rest of the day, okay? I mean, you can talk to us, but no more of that 'girls need protectin' stuff. It's 1983 after all!" Mary nodded in agreement.

I wish I could say that this event cured Nick of his superiority complex or that he began to treat the women in our classes as his equals, but that didn't really happen. He *did* shut up for the rest of the day though, and he didn't, as far as I remember, ever refer to Ed Partington as "Special Ed" again. You're not surprised to hear that he was one of those people, right?

And because he *did* shut up, the rest of the class didn't find out about the falling through the ice and being almost naked in a sleeping bag with Ed. Well, not right away. Kim and Mary kept their words. Neither of them told us over dinner that evening. Nick was uncharacteristically quiet. Because it had been such a great experience for most of us, we all eagerly shared *our* stories, and we didn't really notice that Nick didn't share his.

I'm *guessing* that Nick spent most of that evening and the night that followed worrying that the story would come out, that Kim or Mary or Ed would find it just too delicious to keep to themselves. After what must have been a very bad night for him, over breakfast the next morning, which we all ate together in a very well-appointed large log cabin, he said to the class, "Say, I've been thinking. I listened to everyone's stories last night, and everyone said what a great time they had."

We all agreed.

"I find it a bit unbelievable that *none* of you had a . . . negative incident," he added.

"Well," I answered. "We *did* discover that, for a bit, we'd been walking in the exact opposite direction to what we should have been, but it was for just a few minutes."

"And it *was* kind of funny that Jeremy was *so* frightened by the porcupine!"

"Hey! That thing was huge! How was I supposed to know they don't shoot their quills?"

We all laughed.

Ed Partington took a sip of coffee and said, "You know? A lot of people think porcupines shoot their quills. I guess it's because of the cartoons we watched when we were kids. It's a good thing you didn't try to pet it though. Those quills are sharp!"

Nick looked at Ed, waiting for him to say something else. Then he looked to Mary and Kim, who were smiling at him, but saying nothing.

"Nobody else fell through the ice?" Nick finally blurted out.

"Not us. The maps we were given were really good. I think every stream and brook must've been on them."

"Well *I* did! Could've died, I guess! Right up to my waist. I didn't see the stream because of the fresh snow."

"It was just to your knees, Nick. Don't make it sound worse than it was," Mary stated.

But then, silence, from Kim, Mary, and Ed. They'd promised and were keeping their words. If the story was going to come out, it would have to be from Nick.

And it did.

Nick told us the story with no help from the three other participants. The only part he left out was Kim and Mary flipping a coin to see who would have to get into the sleeping bag with him. Ed emerged as the hero he was. He also established himself firmly as the best outdoor ed teacher any of us would ever know. We toasted him with our coffees and orange juices. Nick actually thanked him for all he'd done.

And to our credit, to *all* of our credits, none of us laughed.

A Job before Teaching

I didn't have many different jobs before I became a teacher. I almost always *had* a job, but I tended to hold on to them for longer than most kids. I delivered flyers throughout grade school. I worked at McDonald's from Grade 11 until I finished my undergraduate degree, saving up enough money so I wouldn't *have* to work while I was in teachers' college. The summer after my first year of working on a master's degree in history, I worked as an archivist for a non-profit organization in a small storefront on one of the main streets in Windsor. This story is about that job.

My job, and I'm not *trying* to make it sound boring, was to go through, catalogue, and arrange all of their myriad papers from almost fifty years of existence, but I was told not to throw *anything* away.

"I can throw away the broken bowling balls though, right?" I asked, looking at the maybe twenty or twenty-five broken-in-half bowling balls piled along the wall. "How does that happen? I've never seen *one* broken bowling ball before, let alone that many."

"I don't know. We'll need to get approval for that from the executive committee," replied the president of the organization. "They're meeting next month. I'll put it on the agenda."

"Because that would give me *some* room to set up a table to work at."

We were talking in the basement of the building. The room was lit by three bare light bulbs hanging from the ceiling. There was literally no way to walk from one end of the basement to the other. The floor was filled with piles of paper. Every flat surface was covered in piles of paper.

"Can I, at least, recycle the papers that have no connection to the organization? Or the duplicates of paper? You really only need to save one copy, the original, of most papers."

"You are not the person to decide that!"

"Ma'am, you *hired* me to decide that."

"Just put all this," she said, waving her arms over the entire basement area, like Moses parting the Red Sea, "just put all this into some semblance of order, and *we* will decide what to throw away and what to keep."

And with that, she ended our conversation and walked back up the stairs.

I worked there for two and a half months, the length of my contract, and I never saw her again. Nor did I hear from the executive committee. I found a table and a couple chairs under all that paper and got to work arranging the papers. But there was just so much garbage in the basement, that it made it impossible for me to do any real work.

I decided to ignore the instructions of the president and began to get rid of the things I knew the organization did not need. I ended up throwing away two or three broken bowling balls a week, so they wouldn't weigh too much and raise the suspicion of the garbage men. I donated the magazines that didn't smell musty to one of the local resale shops and recycled the rest. There were surprisingly few papers that actually had anything to do with the organization, and I was able to organize them relatively easily once I'd dealt with all the material that didn't belong there.

I ate lunch by myself in a park on most days. Every once in a while, I'd treat myself to a sandwich and dill pickle from Virginia's Delicatessen and Sandwich Bar. Usually though, I'd pack myself something and sit on a park bench looking at squirrels or people walking their dogs.

"I've seen you here before . . . How long have you been working for them?" said the man who had just appeared at the other end of the bench.

I'd been very engrossed in the game of tag that two squirrels had been playing and hadn't seen him sit down. He was an older gentleman with a grey moustache. He wore a fedora and a beige raincoat though the sun was shining.

"I'm sorry? Working for whom?"

"That's all right." He smiled and removed his glasses to polish them on a handkerchief. "You don't have to tell me. In fact, I *know* that you won't. There are so many letters in the alphabet, right?"

"I'm sorry. I don't understand." I thought perhaps I just hadn't heard him correctly.

"You're good, kid. I almost believe you. In the end though, it doesn't really matter, does it?" He went quiet for a moment, looking straight ahead and putting his glasses back on.

. For the rest of our conversation, he didn't look at me. "I work for one of the lettered groups too. There are so many of them. FBI, CSIS, CIA . . . I'm not allowed to tell you which one I work for."

As it happened, the non-profit I was working for went by a lettered short form as well, so I told him the letters it went by—still goes by.

"Oh them! You don't look the type, kid. My advice? Get out early. Before they have a chance to chip you. They'll do it while you're sleeping, then they'll be able to track you and send messages which you won't even know are messages. I've gotta get going. On a mission. See you around, kid. Good luck."

I watched him walk away and finished my lunch. Like the executive director of the lettered company I was working for, I never saw him again. I went back to my place of employment, went into the basement, and stuffed three broken bowling balls into an empty box.

Grade 9 Girls Do Not Need to Read That!

You've probably guessed that the short story is one of my preferred forms of writing. I think this has always been the case. If you think back to primary school, it's the way we all start learning to read—I mean, once you get past the alphabet, sounds, and words and sentences. Grade 1's *Mr. Whiskers* and *Magic and Make Believe* are just collections of short stories with the occasional poem thrown in. And despite their length, the Beatrix Potter tales are really just beautifully illustrated short stories.

Chapter books or novels, they come later. Grade 2 or 3 maybe? I love those too. In fact, I love just about all forms of writing, even the occasional textbook. But the short story has always had a special place in my heart.

One of the main reasons, of course, is that you don't have to invest as much time in reading them. Fifteen, twenty minutes—done. On to the next, or put the book down on your night table and go to sleep.

When I was an occasional teacher—a supply teacher— I often had a free half hour that I could devote to a short story or two. There was no planning or marking for me to do. And if there were no supervision scheduled for me, or nothing the principal wanted me to do, then I could go to the library, find a collection of short stories, and experience two, maybe even three of them.

I won't say at which school this story occurred or who the librarian was. It was a very long time ago. Almost forty years. I'm sure she thought she was doing right by her students.

When I looked over my schedule for the day that morning, I saw that, at least on paper, I had a spare just before lunch. I asked the secretary who'd handed me the schedule and the packet of work if there was any supervision for me that day.

"Nope! You're good. Have a nice day. Just bring the key and the packet of work back here at the end of the day or leave the work on the teacher's desk, okay?"

And so, at the beginning of the period before lunch, I made my way to the library. I went to the shelves to look for a particular book: *Welcome to the Monkey House* by Kurt Vonnegut. It's an excellent collection of short stories. In most libraries, it's really easy to find books by

Vonnegut. Fiction is almost always arranged alphabetically by author's last name, and Vonnegut is very near the end of the alphabet.

I was a bit disappointed that *Monkey House* wasn't there, but I was impressed to find that there was no Vonnegut on the shelves at all.

What a great school! I thought. Every single book by Vonnegut has been taken out! Then I thought, Maybe this school library is arranged differently. Maybe the really popular writers are stored somewhere safe, where the librarian can be sure they're loaned out in a fair manner.

I made my way to the card catalogue. (I *said* this happened a long time ago.) I was confused when I found that there were no books by Vonnegut in the catalogue at all.

"May I help you, sir? Are you looking for something in particular?" asked the librarian, a handsome middle-aged woman with eyeglasses on a string, wearing a beige skirt and blouse and beige sensible shoes. In fact, everything about her was beige.

"Yes, thank you. I'm looking for *Welcome to the Monkey House* by Kurt Vonnegut."

She reacted as though I'd smacked her across the face or asked for back issues of *Playboy* magazine. "We have *nothing* by that man!" she spat.

"Not even *Slaughterhouse-Five*?" I asked, incredulous.

"*Especially* not that book! Smut! Grade 9 girls do not need to read that book!"

I was going to answer that they wouldn't. Grade 9 girls and boys wouldn't think of picking it up. They might pick it up when they were a bit older, but I couldn't think of any thirteen-year-old who would read *Slaughterhouse-Five*.

Instead, I said, "It was required reading at my high school, when I was in Grade 12."

"Well, I'm happy to say that that is not the case here! Is there anything else I can help you with?" Her eyes had narrowed, and her lips had become pursed.

I wasn't trying to be a smart ass. I wasn't trying to wind her up. If I'd thought about it at all, I would have asked for almost any other book.

"Do you have *Nine Stories* by J.D. Salinger?" As the words were coming out of my mouth I was thinking, Well *that* was a silly thing to ask for! What's the matter with you? Are you *trying* to give the lady a stroke? I braced myself for whatever she would respond.

For those who may not know, *Slaughterhouse-Five* by Kurt Vonnegut and *The Catcher in the Rye* by J.D. Salinger were among the top most banned books in the United States for the last half of the twentieth century. They are still on most school libraries banned lists if they are the type of libraries that ban such things. It now seemed to me that this was that kind of library.

Instead: "Why, yes, it's right over here." Everything seemed forgiven in her mind. A switch had been thrown, and she returned to being the helpful beige librarian who'd offered to help me in the first place.

I sat down and had the time to enjoy two of my favourite short stories, both of which I taught several times over the course of my career: "A Perfect Day for Bananafish" and "For Esme—with Love and Squalor." I regard both these stories as near perfect, masterpieces of short fiction. I read the first story with great enjoyment but was disappointed that in *For Esme*, someone had defaced the work, blacking out the occasional word with a black marker.

Just before the bell rang for lunch, I approached the librarian to inform her of what I'd found.

"Yes, I know. *I* did that."

"I'm sorry?"

"Obviously, I can't read everything that comes into the library, but when I *know* there will be objectionable content, I remove it before it can be experienced by any of my students. As I said before, Grade 9 girls do not need to read that. I do it to protect them."

I returned to that library hundreds of times over the rest of my career, taking dozens of books off the shelves to read them. I have no idea what happened to the beige librarian, how long she remained at the school or even if she's still alive. I don't even remember her name or remember if I ever knew it. Like the blacked-out words she created in the books she was responsible for, that information has been excised from my memories.

But occasionally, well into this century, when I was a principal, I'd take an older book off the shelf, find a black crossing out, and I'd smile. I'd walk over to the librarian, smile, and tell them my story. As I finished, I'd say, "Do the school a favour: buy a new copy of this book and discard this one, okay? It's been defaced. Grade 9 girls don't need to see that."

Cheryl Donovan

There should be a bit of pathos in this story, and I'm not very good at pathos. I'm good at feeling sorry for people. I'm good at feeling pathos. I'm not very good at writing it.

As I read through Cheryl's obituary, I felt that, even in this last document, she was trying to impress. She was a widow. Older than my mother, with no family. Her husband had died seven years before she had, she had no children, and the obituary didn't mention any nieces or nephews or brothers or sisters. In all the time I'd known her, she'd never spoken of family.

So, she'd written her own obituary.

It said she was an English teacher for more than forty-four years. I knew she had the papers that *said* she was a teacher of English, but in all the time I'd known her, she was an occasional teacher—a supply teacher. From the first time I met her, I knew that she would always be a supply teacher. She would never be hired to teach her own classes. In fact, I doubted she'd ever be given a long-term assignment.

The obit also said she'd been elected to the International Poetry Hall of Fame, which, I have to admit, did impress me, until I googled it to find that it wasn't really, well, real.

It exists, if you look it up, but it's quite clearly a joke, dedicated to "Emmett Lee Dickinson, Emily Dickinson's third cousin, twice removed, at her request." For a few seconds, I thought that maybe Cheryl had a sense of humour but then thought better of it. I'd never even seen Cheryl *smile,* let alone crack a joke. Nope. It was far more likely that someone had told Cheryl she'd been elected, and she'd simply believed it to the point she included it in her obituary.

I didn't doubt that she wrote poetry under the pen name Dusty Rose Boudoir, as the obituary claimed, and that it was heavily influenced by the words of Robert Frost and Robbie Burns. But I also knew that the poetry would be punishment to read.

Despite all this, I'll miss her, and I credit her with getting me hired as a contract teacher. I'd have caught on eventually, and maybe I'm giving Cheryl Donovan more credit than she deserves, but I *believe* I was hired because of her.

Cheryl always wore the same outfit to school. Every day, every season. She may have had a number of pairs of the black winter boots with black faux-fur fringe that never seemed to leave her feet, and I'm sure she had a number of the black skirts and white shirts, but they were always the same. Her hair, too, never changed. She wore it in the same fashion as Moe from the Three Stooges. Despite her age, it was always jet black, almost as if treated with shoe polish.

The kids called her Mrs. Boots. Even after she told them her name and wrote it on the board. Somehow, the nickname followed her from school to school. I found that very interesting and would sometimes comment on it in staffrooms.

"How do you think that happens?" I'd ask.

This was before the internet and social media. No one could offer a reasonable explanation.

"Kids notice things, you know," someone would say.

"Yes, but wouldn't you notice the hair? Wouldn't you figure out something to say about that instead? Call her Mrs. Howard? Ask her, maybe, how her brother Curly's doing? And how does the name 'Mrs. Boots' travel from school to school?"

Obviously, this was never when Cheryl Donovan was in the room.

She was smart but not . . . capable. She got the work done that was left for her by the teacher, and the kids, mostly, left her alone.

I remember once, though, I was walking down the hall while class was going on. I didn't even know that Cheryl was in the school that day. A girl almost fell into the hall from a classroom and into my arms. Blood was streaming down her arm, and she looked as though she was going to faint.

"What happened to you? Let's get you to the office!"

"Jordan Nuttal stabbed me on accident! He didn't mean to!"

She leaned against me as we worked our way to the office as quickly as we could. Fortunately, Vickie Oglan was in the office and saw that the girl was at risk of going into shock. She sat the girl down, who was beginning to shake uncontrollably, and told me to get the first aid kit.

The girl was holding her right hand, as tightly as she could, in her left.

"Are you cut, hon?" asked Vickie.

The girl nodded.

"Are there guts and everything?"

The girl started laughing. It's much harder to go into shock if you're laughing. Vickie was masterful at dealing with such things, and while she was getting the girl bandaged up, who wasn't cut that badly, I went to get Jordan Nuttal.

The whole reason I'm telling you this story is that the accidental stabbing, the girl leaving the room bleeding, and Dave Garlick getting Jordan Nuttal out of the class and down to the office, all happened in a class being supervised by Cheryl Donovan, who was reading the newspaper at the teacher's desk while the class worked quietly.

Jordan had taken out his pen knife and was pretending he was going to cut the girl's binder. He and the girl had been quietly laughing about it, each enjoying the joke, when she went to grab her binder as he moved forward with the knife. He stabbed her between the fingers but didn't even realize what had happened. He stopped laughing when he *understood* what had happened but, at thirteen, was too immature to offer her his help.

She left the room, found me, and got herself tended to.

I went back to the room, stuck my head in the room and motioned to Jordan to come with me.

Cheryl never realized any of that happened.

That's not what she did that got me hired. Neither was it the time she drove me home from school when my car broke down, as it often did in the 1980s.

I was quick to accept the offer from Cheryl, not just because I was grateful for the help and needed the ride, but more because I found Cheryl fascinating and knew the ride home would be an adventure. It was December. It had either snowed earlier that week, or was going to snow the next week. What I mean to say is that there was no actual snow on the ground, but the *idea* of snow was present.

It took us about fifteen minutes to get from the back door of the school to the parking lot and Cheryl's car. This was, maybe, a hundred yards. She traversed that distance as though she was climbing Everest. She refused my arm in favour of the fence around the tennis courts, moving painfully slowly.

"Are you sure you can't hold onto my arm, Cheryl?"

"Men have been known to fall, Mr. Garlick. Even young, strong men like yourself, and I won't have you dragging me to a broken hip and a slow, painful death," she answered.

When we finally got close enough to Cheryl's car so that I could see inside it, I realized that there was a man in the back seat. He opened Cheryl's door for her from the back seat and said, "I'm sorry, honeybunch! I've fogged up the back seat waiting for you!"

"That's no problem, sweet knees, but you'll have to wipe it off before we can leave. Mr. Garlick will be sitting next to me." Cheryl looked at me and explained, "Gerry doesn't drive, and he prefers to sit in the back seat."

Over the years, I've wondered how Gerry Donovan came to be in the back seat of the car. Had he waited there all day for her in the cold? Had he walked there from home for the exercise? For the Cheryl Donovan I've created in my mind in the years since meeting her, I prefer to think he'd waited for her in the car. In any case, we couldn't begin to leave the parking lot until every inch of the back window was free of the Gerry-induced fog.

"There's still a little in the corner, bottom left. No, my left," Cheryl instructed.

We then drove home at a pace that was only marginally faster than the way she'd traversed the parking lot.

I smiled the whole way.

"Cheryl, you're on the negotiating committee with Dave," my wife said. "There can't *be* any emergencies that would mean you'd have to call us after nine at night. For me, an emergency is one of our parents being sick. Okay? It's an emergency if one of their houses catches fire. Nothing can happen while you're negotiating that's an *emergency*. You can call up until nine o'clock, but not after."

Linda hung up the phone. "I'm sorry, Dave, but I've got to be firm with her. This is crazy. It's ten thirty! And there's no such thing as an unjust cause clause!"

"A what?" I asked.

"I don't know. Maybe she didn't say that. She wanted to talk to you about the brief."

"We're meeting after school tomorrow. Anything she needs to tell me about the brief she can tell me then."

"That's what I told her, and she agreed! But then she added that she might have to call you in the case of an emergency! I will be *so* happy when this contract is signed!"

Cheryl and I were on the Occasional Teachers' Negotiating Committee together for the group's first contract. I was chief negotiator and Cheryl, with a law degree, was also on the committee. For the last couple weeks, she'd been calling me daily. By this time, Cheryl was a widow, and although Cheryl may have pretended the issues were important, I knew she was really calling because she was lonely, and this committee was filling her time and giving her a sense of importance.

The next day, though, our meeting started like this: "I'm glad to see that you've put a just cause clause in our brief, David, but you have to add an unjust cause clause."

This was our last meeting before actually negotiating with the Board. Cheryl sounded both intelligent and reasonable. And while there is no doubt that she was intelligent, she was often less than reasonable.

The *just* cause clause was a statement that called on the Board to agree that they would never fire a teacher unless they had "just cause," meaning a good reason. Such clauses were pretty standard in most contracts, and this was something that the Board would have no problem agreeing with. It was no more controversial or problematic than the statement that the Windsor Public Board of Education would, after the first time it was mentioned in our brief, be referred to as "the Board."

"Pardon?" I asked. I remembered what Linda had said the night before, and she'd been correct. Cheryl *had* mentioned an unjust cause clause.

"We need an unjust cause clause. The Board needs to agree that they won't fire somebody for an unjust cause."

"That's the same thing as a just cause clause. The Board needs a good reason to fire somebody. That means a bad reason, or an unjust reason won't do," I countered, thinking maybe I was missing something.

"With all due respect *Mister* Garlick, you're very much in error. Without an unjust cause clause, the Board will simply use bad reasons to fire people."

"Cheryl, if the Board agrees that they have to have *just* cause to fire somebody, that also means they are agreeing that *un*just reasons are not acceptable, right?" I'd changed my wording slightly, as well as the emphasis I placed on certain words, in the same way when talking to the one or two students that didn't understand a concept the first time I'd change my explanations a bit, which usually sufficed.

"Let's read through the rest of the brief and come back to this, okay? I'm pretty busy," she said.

We read through the rest of the brief, and remark-ably, she found no other issues with any of it. Pay scale, working conditions, how teachers would be called out in the mornings—all agreed to without comment. By now it was 8:30 p.m., and we all wanted to get home, because actual negotiations were set to begin the next morning.

"Let's go back to the need for an unjust cause clause, David. Just admit that you're wrong and we can go home."

"I'll tell you what, Cheryl. If you want one so badly, we'll put it in, but I will resign, you will be chief negotia-tor, and you'll get to present the brief and you will—"

"I don't want you to resign!"

"And I don't want to resign. But I'm tired of explaining this to you. And with regard to admitting that I'm wrong, no, I won't do that in this case, because I'm not, in this case. And if I stay on as chief negotiator there will be no unjust cause clause, and if you so much as mention it tomorrow when we begin negotiations, I will shut things down, walk out, and resign, and you will have to take over. Do I have your understanding?"

"Yes, sir."

"Then we're done here. Good night, everyone. Let's meet very briefly tomorrow morning at 7:30 before we go into negotiations. Get a good night's sleep."

Mary Jean Gallagher had sat there quietly throughout the entire meeting, not offering her opinion or helping me in any way, but I'd been careful not to ask for her help or opinion either. I noticed her smile when I threatened to resign though, and then smile and nod when I said, "Do I have your understanding?"

Mary Jean was the president of the union and a principal in our board.

I forget whether Mary Jean was actually with us when we started negotiating the next morning. She probably was, but she'd taught me so effectively that it didn't make any difference. I knew what to expect. I was confident in our brief, and I was as ready for this as I'd ever been ready for anything.

The chief negotiator for the Board appeared to lose his mind. He threw our brief on the ground and told me if I expected to achieve any of it, I was "dreaming in technicolour." He called my intelligence into question. He didn't swear, which actually disappointed me. When he'd finished, I smiled.

"Are we ready to begin now?" I asked.

I forget almost everything about the sessions that led to that first contract. I don't even remember how many times we met. It may have been only once. It may have taken two or three meetings. I do remember the Board's chief negotiator reaching across the table and shaking my hand.

And I remember, early on, reading the part that dealt with the just cause clause. I read it out loud, looked at Cheryl, not the negotiator, and said, "Do you have any issues with this section?" Cheryl and the negotiator responded, "No" at the same time, surprising both him and Cheryl.

I was the only person there not surprised.

I was given a contract the following September, working at the same school as Mary Jean Gallagher. Although we've never spoken about it, I'm certain, thirty-three years later, that it was more about how I'd handled Cheryl Donovan that evening than how I'd handled any of the students I'd worked with in the years before that.

RIP Cheryl Donovan.

Directions: 1992–94

Is this a dagger which
I see before me.

In June of 1993, I knew for the first time in my ten-year career in education that I had a job in September and at what school I was going to be working. I was going to be at Directions for the second year. Directions was a small program of twenty kids, two teachers, and a youth worker.

When I'd started there, Val Pistor "sold" the program to me in this manner:

"Dave, we want—no, *need*—you to work with these kids. There's only going to be twenty of them, but for various reasons, they're not buying into the regular program. They've become disengaged. Your job will be to help re-engage them. Get them excited about coming to school, get them some success, and then get them back to regular school."

"Why aren't they buying in?" I asked.

"As I said, for various reasons." Val thought for a few seconds. "Some are just too bright for their classmates. Some have been excluded from their home schools." (I was unfamiliar with that word as it applied to kids and school, but it sounded similar to expelled and that wasn't good.) "One student just got addicted to skipping out, so there was no point in him going back to his school at that point in the semester. None of them are *bad* kids, really."

No matter what Val said, I was going to take the job. He and I both knew it. I was still a young teacher and in July of 1992, I had *no* job prospects. I'd been declared redundant from both my school board and the separate school board. If you're unfamiliar with the word "redundant," it's almost as bad as a word can be for a young teacher. It means there's no prospect of a job for you, anywhere, in September. Maybe if a few teachers have heart attacks over the summer, or something similarly tragic occurs, but it would probably be smart for you to look into another profession, or another city.

But I'd gotten lucky, and it didn't even involve a heart attack or someone's death, and I was being offered a position in a special program. No one else in the system wanted the position.

Directions was a great little program. Val was right. There weren't any bad kids. In fact, there were some pretty great kids. They were each just twenty individual challenges. There was one kid, Sandy, who was too bright for her classmates. At fifteen, she was a tough little thing, and she'd built up a series of walls to hide that brightness from her teachers and her peers.

There were three or four kids who *thought* they were bad kids—kids who thought they were on the path to be bad adults, and although maybe they were on that path, none of them turned out that way.

"Sorry, sir, I wasn't in class last week, I was inside," said one of my "ne'er-do-wells" on a Monday morning.

"Inside what?" I asked.

"Jail. The pokey," he responded with a bit of pride.

This got everyone's attention around the table. "What did you do?" asked one of my not ne'er-do-wells.

"Robbed the corner store. Stupid owner fingered me to the cops."

"You robbed the corner store—your own corner store? The one you live down the street from?" I asked.

"Yeah."

"Were you wearing a mask or anything? A disguise?" asked Sandy.

"No."

"Well, *that* was pretty stupid. What, are you a complete frickin' idiot?" Sandy said this completely matter-of-factly, as though she was asking to borrow a pencil.

"That's what the cop said, too."

Sandy finished off the conversation. "You know what? Maybe you should just try harder in school. Listen to Dave and Bill and Bob. Maybe get a few credits and graduate. Crime isn't for you."

That's what ended up happening—to that kid and the two others who stole their mother's car one night and ran from the police because that's what they'd seen on TV, so they knew that's what they were supposed to do. All of them graduated and became productive members of society. Our youth criminal justice system does work pretty well, as long as everyone stays patient, waits a few years, and there's a Sandy in class.

Schools throughout Windsor sent us their most difficult fourteen- and fifteen-year-olds, the kids no one could reach. Each school sent us one, two, or three of them. Each school knew that every other school was sending us a few of the same sort of kid. So even though the other teacher in the program, Bill Miller, our child and youth worker, Bob Glass, and I never had a bad word to say about the program, everybody in the system knew, or thought they knew, what our program was like.

Anyway, back to June of 1993. I'd been at Directions for a year, and as I said, I knew that I was staying there. To finish up the year, Bill, Bob, and I decided to take the kids to the beach. We rented a school bus, and around seventeen kids loaded themselves onto it. Bob joined them. Bill and I followed them in Bill's car.

We had the food, the drinks, the barbecue, and the charcoal. We had the games and the sunscreen and the sun-umbrellas.

About half an hour from the city, it hit me, and I started to laugh.

"What's so funny?" Bill asked.

"We're on the way to the beach."

"Yeah, I still don't see what's so funny. The trip was approved by our principal."

"We're on the way to the beach, and we're getting paid to go."

"It's a learning experience, Dave. We've been over this. And some of these kids have never even *been* to a beach."

"We're on the way to the beach. We're getting paid to go, and there isn't a single teacher in the system who wanted to bump me out of this job!"

Bill and I laughed for the rest of the way to the beach.

The following September, no one at Directions laughed when I said I wanted to take the kids to Stratford. Bill and Bob both thought it was a great idea. Bill would have preferred the Shaw Festival, something by Gilbert and Sullivan, but Stratford was a good choice too. *Macbeth* was on the playbill, and I thought that would be an excellent introduction to the theatre.

"I'll take the kids who are taking English this semester."

Here's how Directions worked: I taught English, history, geography, French, and phys ed. Bill taught math, science, business, and phys ed. The kids took whatever courses they needed, but they were correspondence courses. Each course was twenty lessons long, and if they did one lesson a week, with either Bill or me helping them when they needed it or asked for help, they would get a credit in a semester, in each of those courses. No one would bug them, and if they worked to that schedule, they would get four credits each semester, just like regular school.

But here's how we were different. If the kid *wanted to*, they could do *more* than one lesson a week. They could do two, three, or four. They could not only catch up to their peers in regular school, but they could also get ahead of them.

If the kids were having difficulties outside of school, say with a parent, a sibling, or a friend, they would ask to speak with Bob, our youth worker, and Bill and I would always say, "Yes, go ahead." This was unusual in 1992 and 1993. It probably still is in regular schools, but why would we say, "No"?

Another major difference between Directions and regular school was that Mr. Miller, the fifty-year-old, brush-cutted, straight-as-an-arrow teacher, was just "Bill" to the kids. Mr. Glass, the fifty-year-old, ponytailed, almost-certainly-a-hippy-in-the-'60s youth worker was just "Bob" and I was just "Dave." At first, the kids thought that this was insane, but Bill, Bob, and I worked really hard not to answer to "sir" or "mister" or "Hey, you." "My name is Dave or David, and that's all I expect you to call me, okay?"

Those few differences worked like magic for most kids. We had fewer discipline problems than regular school. Kids did get re-engaged in their education. Most got caught up with their peers, and a few did get ahead. The only thing we never got any good at was getting them excited about going back to their former, or *any*, regular school. We were just *different*, and although Bob was far better at helping the kids work through their difficulties outside of school, the kids knew that Bill and I cared too and that we'd offer them the best advice we could, if we were asked.

So when I held a program meeting to see how many kids wanted to go to Stratford, I got few of the answers or questions a regular teacher would get. Some of them had no interest in going, more intent on their math or science or business courses. Some had no interest in seeing Shakespeare on stage. "Before I got kicked out, they tried to teach me Shakespeare. *Romeo and Juliet*. I didn't get it. Thee and thou and thus. Maybe when I'm older . . ."

But many of the kids asked and said things like, "What's the play about, Dave?" "Do you really think I'll like it?" "If *you* say I'll get it, I trust you."

They balked a bit at having to get a little dressed up. I told them, "This is the *theatre,* guys. It's a bit of a deal. It's not like going to the movies. And it's one of the best theatres in the world! Wearing a pair of nice pants and a shirt with a collar is not too much to ask, is it?"

Grudgingly, "I guess not."

I explained the plot to the whole group of kids, the difference between a tragedy, a comedy, and a history. I explained the concepts of a tragic hero and a tragic flaw. I told them their job was going to be able to tell me what they thought Macbeth's flaw was. I told them that I was not giving anything away when I told them Macbeth dies at the end.

"Everyone who's ever gone to see the play for five hundred years has known Macbeth was going to die.

That's the point of a tragedy. You've got to figure out *why* he dies."

They thought the witches were cool.

Eight of the kids signed up right away. "You might have to call my father to explain why we're missing a day of school, but I think he'll let me go."

"My mom too."

"My gramma will just be happy I'm gone for the day."

Getting the signed parental consent forms was just as difficult as at a regular school. Some kids just can't seem to remember. And some parents just can't seem to see the importance of these things.

Every day, I'd tell them a little more about the theatre, Stratford, the day I'd planned, or the play. Even some of the kids who weren't going wanted to hear about it. And even though some of the kids threatened to show up in jeans and a t-shirt, I could tell they were excited, and I was surprised when I found out that some of the kids had never even left Essex County and this would be the longest trip of their lives so far.

To save money, I'd rented a van instead of a school bus. I would drive. Linda, my wife, would go along as a chaperone, and eight kids would pile into the van at 7:30 in the morning, an hour and a half before school started for everybody else in the program and almost everybody else in the city.

No one was late. All eight of the kids looked sharp. No one complained and there was none of the usual, "I want the back seat! I want a window!" The kids just piled in, and we actually left early.

The first question of the day was not something I'd anticipated. "Dave? Are we going to see any wildlife on the way?"

"Well, I don't know. What do you mean by wildlife?"

"You know, horses? Cows? I've never actually seen one of them, in real life."

"Oh yes, then. We're going to see all kinds of wildlife!"

So discussions about *Macbeth* were interrupted by comments like: "Oh my God! Those are goats!" "I didn't know that cows could be brown and white too. I've only ever seen pictures of the black and white ones." And "Many people think that cows have four stomachs, but they don't. They've got one with four compartments. Bill told me that."

When we finally got to Stratford, even though the kids knew it was going to happen when I parked the van and released them for the rest of the morning, they hung around Linda and me at first.

"Listen, Linda and I are going to go to a gardening store, okay? You do *not* want to be with us. The play starts at 1:00. I've told you where the shops are, and the restaurants, if you want to go to one of them. I know you've each got enough money for lunch, and I've given you each a map of the town. Meet me outside the theatre at 12:45, and I'll give you your tickets, okay?

"Would it be okay if I stayed with you and Linda, Dave? I don't feel safe by myself, and I don't want to hang out with the other kids. I don't mind going to a gardening store. Of course, if you don't want me to . . ."

This was Sandy, the girl I mentioned at the beginning of the story. The tough one, with so many walls. But now, less than a year later, there were almost no walls. She was just a really bright, but very . . . fragile kid. One who could beat the heck out of anyone who challenged her to but would also cry about it that night.

"Sure, Sandy. You can hang out with Linda and me. Don't tell any of the other kids, but first, we're going to the best toy store you've ever seen! And then a great bookstore!"

An hour later, we accidentally met up with the rest of the kids, who yelled at us from across the street. "Hey Dave! We've got a bone to pick with you! A major bone! This town sucks! There's nothing to do! There's not even a pool hall!"

Linda smiled. "We'll be sure to take that up with the town council, okay?"

But Sandy added, "Are you kidding? Have you *been* to the toy store? They let me fire off a rocket in the *street*! And I found a used copy of Edgar Lee Masters's *Spoon River Anthology* for three bucks! This place is frickin' amazing! The toy store is just up the street. Dave, Linda, and I will see you in an hour. Have a good time, chumps!"

By the time we took our seats in the theatre, all ten of us, no one late, we all agreed that Stratford was a pretty cool place.

I sat between Linda and Sandy. Francine sat next to Linda. Francine was a different sort of kid. We all knew that she belonged at Directions. She'd fallen behind her peers at her home school and stopped attending. I wouldn't use the word "simple" to describe her, but it works. She ended up graduating like the rest of her classmates, but she always seemed to be, mentally at least, somewhere else. A nice kid though. Just before the play was to start, she leaned over and whispered to Linda, "Dave's been really patient with me, so I don't want to ask him. I just don't get it."

"Get what?" Linda asked.

"*Macbeth*. Well, not the whole play, but Lady Macbeth. I don't get her."

"What do you mean?"

"Well, who *is* she?

"I don't understand. She's Macbeth's wife."

"Oh! You mean, she's *Mrs*. Macbeth?"

"Yes."

"Oh! Now I get it! I get the whole play now! Thanks! Gee. Mrs. Macbeth!"

The kids were great through the play. The play was wonderful. The witches were cool. Duncan, Banquo, Lady Macbeth, and finally Macbeth all died, just the way the kids knew they would. And the kids loved it. They were the first to jump to their feet to give the actors a standing ovation.

"Are all Shakespeare's plays that good, Dave?" "I was so surprised when the actors came out for their bows at the end. I almost thought they'd really been killed!" "I didn't find it hard to understand at all!" "Macbeth was *gorgeous*! What's his real name, Dave?" "It says here in the program that his name is Scott Wentworth." "Yeah? Well, he's gorgeous!" Those were the questions and comments in the van all the way home.

Without me even getting involved in the discussion, they tried to figure out Macbeth's tragic flaw. "Do you think he just wanted to be king too badly?"

"It could be that he put too much faith in what the witches told him."

"Maybe he should have been able to stand up to his wife and do the right thing."

"If he hadn't killed Duncan, none of the bad stuff would have ended up happening."

I was a very proud teacher on the way home. Even more so the next morning, when the kids told Bill, Bob, and the students who'd stayed behind all about the day.

"Dave left us alone all morning!"

"He trusted us by ourselves!"

"None of us were even a minute late!"

"The play was fantastic!"

"I feel sorry for you guys that weren't there!"

"Scott Wentworth as Macbeth is frickin' gorgeous!"

"There were cows and horses and goats and hawks, and I'm pretty sure I saw a couple deer."

I helped make all that happen in a school that no other teacher wanted to work in. But to be fair to them, they had no idea what Directions was really all about.

"And just in case you didn't know it, Dave's wife told me that Lady Macbeth was really *Mrs.* Macbeth!"

Performance Appraisals as a Teacher and a Principal, and Friendships

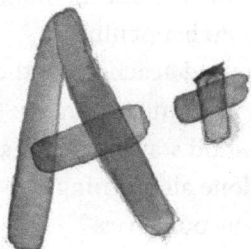

I've never been a fan of teacher performance appraisals; not as a teacher, nor as a principal. I remember a superintendent saying to us, at a principals' meeting, that good teachers actually looked forward to them. It gives them the chance to show off their skills and be recognized for the good teachers they are.

"Well, I must never have been a good teacher then," I said to myself, and probably to the table of principals I was sitting with. As a teacher, I hated performance appraisals. I lost sleep. I spent days tweaking a written lesson plan I only created because I was being evaluated. I knew that a few years after I'd left teachers' college, all the terminology

I was taught to use had become passé. "Objectives" had become "expectations," for example, and everything became far more student centred than teacher centred. While this was a good thing, it also pointed out to me that I was getting older, and I worried that my lesson plan would point that out to the principal before they even got to my room.

Only once in the years before I became an administrator did I actually enjoy the process. Warwick Mercer just arrived at my door one morning and asked if he could sit in on my class. "The kids have been telling me how much they like you, and I just want to see why for myself, okay? If you don't want me to, I understand."

Of course, I invited him in.

It was a senior class, but I have no memories of what it was that I was teaching that day. Mr. Mercer took part, I remember that. He asked questions and made comments like any other kid in the class. I remember too that he stuck around for a few minutes after the class was over at the beginning of lunch.

"Well, that was fun! Dave, neither of the VPs can remember you ever sending a student to them. They said that you probably handle all your discipline yourself. Is that the case?"

"I don't know . . . I can't think of a time I *needed* to discipline a student here."

"And why do you suppose that is? Do you just put up with bad behaviour?"

"No, I just treat the kids like, well, potential friends, I guess. I treat them the *way* I treat my friends. All students,

David Garlick

juniors and seniors both, seem to appreciate being treated as adults."

A week later, my performance appraisal appeared in my mailbox at school. I hadn't even realized I was being evaluated. More than twenty-five years later, I remember two things about the written report. He started it by writing, "Mr. Garlick's transfer to this school represents the best trade we've had this century." The hyperbole of that sentence, written in 1995, has always amused me, but made me proud at the same time.

He went on to say, "Mr. Garlick has very few issues with classroom discipline. In part this is due to his engaging teaching style, but mostly because he treats all his students as potential friends. No one wants to create problems for a friend."

Now, here's a pretty interesting thing: in my thirty-three-year career, I worked with close to ten thousand students. And now, as a retiree, although I'm *friendly* with all of them, there are only four or five that I really consider to be friends; people I've been out to dinner with, or had them over for an evening, or been invited to their homes. (I'm not fishing for invites here, by the way.) But maybe that's not the best way to define friendship anyway. I consider a lot of the teachers, administrators, superintendents, and directors I worked with as friends, but I've been to very few of their homes, nor have many been to mine. Those who have, I guess, I consider to be *close* friends.

But even that's not right. Looking back, there are a lot of kids and teachers and administrators that I *love*. If they were to call me up to ask for something, I'd be there for them in a heartbeat, and they'd be there for me. Perhaps that's how friendship is best defined. I haven't seen many of them in years, but it's still true. So maybe those *potential* friends did become friends after all.

Performance Appraisals as a Principal

As I mentioned above, I never was a fan of performance appraisals when I was a teacher, and things did not improve in that regard when I became a principal. Perhaps they would have improved if I'd been allowed to conduct them like Warwick Mercer had conducted mine. Just drop in, take part in the lesson, make a few kids laugh, learn a few things, have a good time, *then* tell the teacher they were being evaluated. Avoid all the nervousness and the fake written lesson plan for a lesson they would not have taught in the first place. I would have watched the lesson that was *supposed* to take place that day. And the thing was, teachers never minded having me in their class. I was fun!

If I'd been in a school for more than a year, teachers knew that I just dropped in occasionally. They expected it, and sometimes they'd ask me to stop by: "Dave, you've *got* to see this. It's a great lesson!"

But you couldn't do appraisals like that. You had to let the teacher know within so many days of the start of the school year that this would be a year they'd get evaluated. You had to tell them what you'd be looking for and ask them what else they'd like for you to look for. The idea, I guess, was to make them a partner in the process. Then you had to give them something like two weeks' warning as to when, exactly, you'd be there to watch the class. Then you had to meet with them before the appraisal, hold the appraisal, meet with them after the appraisal, prepare the report, meet with them about the report, get them to sign the report, photocopy the report, give a copy to the teacher, keep a copy for the school, and send a copy to the Human Resources Department at the school board office, and you only had so much time to do all this. I forget what the timeline was. Often, I didn't get it completed on time and asked the teachers involved to lie with me about the dates.

I'm not making excuses, but I was never very good at getting the reports completed on time. I found the reports unwieldy. I resented having to learn how to fill out the digital form, which always seemed to change a little bit from year to year. I was good at holding the meetings, and usually pretty good about being in the classroom for the whole period, but following through with completing the report . . . well . . .

"Okay, sign here and date it, but please, write February 7, okay?"

"You mean March 7, don't you?" asked the teacher sitting across from me.

"Nope. We've got to lie or start the whole thing over again. I took too much time to get this to you."

"Oh . . . February 7 it is."

The Walkie-Talkie

"Walkie-talkie" is a silly name, when you think about it, but it says what it is, and I don't know a single principal or vice-principal who'd try to go more than a few hours without one. Make sure it's charged up, clip it on your belt, and you're ready to go. Literally.

You can leave the school, walk the neighbourhood, go into that alley where you've been told the kids are smoking pot at lunch, go visit the neighbour whose black dog had a white stripe painted along his back (really!) to apologize, and see if there was anything that could be done to fix the situation.

You can do all that, and your secretary, vice-principal, or custodian can contact you immediately.

As a principal, I had huge respect for the devices. Those with rechargeable batteries lasted all day before they had to be recharged, and they weren't very expensive. Huge respect.

As a teacher though, before becoming an administrator, I saw them as a sort of affectation, I guess. Principals wore them, I thought, the way a wannabe gunslinger wore a six-shooter in the Wild West. More for show than anything else. Something to make them *look* important.

And so, when Warwick Mercer asked Bonnie Fraser, Danny Bonk, and me to watch over the school one afternoon when he and the vice-principals were needed at a meeting of all the principals and vice-principals, I was happy to help, but I saw the issuing of walkie-talkies to us as unnecessary and as silly as the name.

In my mind, I thought back to the days of two tin cans connected by thirty feet of string, holding your ear to one can, while your friend whispered, "You're an idiot, Garlick," to see if it really worked.

Your friend found out when you whispered back, "So are you, dumbass."

"Cool!" We both said at the same time despite the insults.

But we were eleven then. And now I was in my late thirties, Bonnie fifteen years older than I was, and Danny probably the same. What were we doing with these things?

Anyway, our instructions for the afternoon were simple. Wander around the entire school. Make sure the halls were reasonably empty of kids. Ask any kids we *did* see why they weren't in class, and check outside the building occasionally. Use the walkie-talkies to stay in touch with one another and the office. Press the talk button to talk. Let go of it to listen. Easy.

When Danny Bonk was given his, he ran to the other side of the room, about twenty feet away, and said in a clear voice, "Can you hear me from way over here?" We laughed, but then he asked Warwick, "Seriously, though, what kind of range do these things have?"

"I'm not really sure. I've taken them to the corner and down Erie Street though, and they work at least that far."

"Impressive," said Danny. "Maybe I'll just take it home and call in from there."

I whispered into mine, "Danny, you're an idiot."

"Hey! I heard that!" said Danny.

"Cool!" I smiled.

Then Warwick left, leaving Danny, Bonnie, and me in charge. This was the first time any of us had been responsible for any part of the building larger than our classrooms.

We decided to split into two groups. Bonnie and I were one group. Danny was a group of his own.

Bonnie and I spoke to maybe three kids in the next half hour. Danny said he saw less than that.

"A well-oiled machine," Bonnie reasoned.

The walkie-talkies *were* kind of fun though. I started pretending it was a CB radio.

"Breaker, breaker. Catch you on the flip side."

The three of us were having a great afternoon.

Then Danny started singing into his walkie-talkie. Danny was an accomplished musician and had been part of several bands over the years, so he was actually pretty good. Far better than Bonnie or me.

"Do you know any Bob Seger? I like Bob Seger," Bonnie requested.

Danny broke into a passable version of "Old Time Rock and Roll," but when he stopped to take a breath, someone broke in: "Who is playing on these walkie-talkies? Who do you think you are?"

Bonnie was sure that it was Danny, a floor or two away, pulling our legs.

She put one hand on her hip and spoke into her device. "It's Bonnie Fraser and David Garlick, Daniel Bonk! Who do you think it is? And who do you think *you* are if I may be so bold to ask?"

"This is Todd Beckett at the Adult Learning Centre on Ottawa Street. Stop playing with those things or I'll report you to your principal!"

Bonnie looked both shocked and guilty at the same time. "Geesh! We'd better stop, or we'll get ourselves in trouble."

"What can they do to us? Tell us we can't do this again? Take away our walkie-talkie privileges?"

Then Danny came up the stairs from the main floor. Bonnie and I had been on the second.

"Beckett's a bit of a jerk, isn't he? Killjoy. I've never liked the guy. I was just getting warmed up! Is there something else you'd like to hear, Mrs. Fraser?"

"Maybe we should just do our jobs for the next hour or so. Not get into trouble. Cool it with the walkie-talkies?" Bonnie suggested, in an almost pleading voice. "I really thought it was you!"

"I guess we should stop playing around. They've got quite the range though, eh?" said Danny. "Geez! All the way to Ottawa Street from here!"

And so, we split up again. Bonnie and I went outside, and Danny went up to the third floor and the tech wing. For the next hour or so, we were responsible part time administrators. No goofing around on the walkie-talkies. Well, not too much.

Near the end of the day, Bonnie and I came in from outside, and saw Danny at the end of the hallway by the main office. He waved to us and then went through the door into the office, and then he began to sing "(I Can't Get No) Satisfaction" by the Rolling Stones. Bonnie and I both laughed as we walked the hallway towards the office. But then—

"I warned you! I am going to report you to your principal and your superintendent! Bonnie Fraser, Danny Bonk, and David Garlick! You are in a world of trouble!"

We walked into the office to find a very sorry looking Danny Bonk. "Sorry you two! I mean, I knew that Beckett was a *bit* of a jerk, but still . . . I've never liked the guy!"

"There's nothing really to worry about," I said. "What can they do to us? And for what, really?"

Then Danny picked up his walkie-talkie which he'd placed on the counter and said, "Garlick, you're right! And Beckett is a complete and *total* jerk!" He put his walkie-talkie to his mouth and said, dismissively, "Bite me, Beckett!"

From all three of our walkie-talkies, now together in the main office, and from the secretaries' walkie-talkies, came a long litany of loud invective. Danny looked proud. Bonnie looked shocked and frightened. I wasn't sure if I should laugh or not. I envisioned Warwick Mercer the next day saying to us in the office, "Well, *you* three aren't doing *that* together again!"

Then I looked at the end of the office hallway—and saw our afternoon custodian shouting into his walkie-talkie, doing a very good impression of Todd Beckett, I guess, who neither Bonnie nor I had ever met, and whose office was actually, when we thought about it, way too far away for walkie-talkies to carry, and who was actually supposed to be at the same meeting as Warwick and our vice-principals.

When our custodian saw that I'd seen him, he stopped threatening us, started laughing, and said, again into the walkie-talkie, "Bonk put me up to it!"

I started laughing as did Danny and the secretaries. It took Bonnie a few seconds to understand what had been happening all afternoon, but then she joined in the laughter as well. "Todd Beckett" had always been our custodian. When Danny was singing "Old Time Rock and Roll," he'd been in the main office, serenading the secretaries.

It was the best practical joke I'd ever been the victim of. It was hilarious! Even now, almost thirty years later, I still find it funny. But until Danny was transferred, and Bonnie retired, every once in a while, out of nowhere, Bonnie would say to me, "We still need to get Danny Bonk back, you know. We've *got* to get him back!"

Part Three:
David as Vice-Principal and Principal

Vignettes

A while ago, back in the introduction, I told you about my "barebones incidents"— short, two- or three-sentence reminders of things that happened to me over the course of my career. Most of what you've read, in this book, has been culled from those things.

Please understand, a lot of those incidents were not funny at all. They have titles like "A Bad Day," "A Really Bad Day," or "Called the Police Again." I don't think I'll ever write about those things. It's hard enough for me to re-read them. I don't want you to have to read them as well.

But there are some really good ones that I can't figure out how to turn into full length stories yet. I think that you'll enjoy reading about some of them though.

Here goes—

Jesse

At the end of a particularly trying day, which included some bad stuff I won't bother you with, I was returning to my office, worn down by the responsibilities of the job. It was November or December. A young man was waiting outside my office. I recognized him, but we hadn't spoken much. I was the vice-principal, and he was a really good kid.

I put on the best tired-but-how-can-I-help-you-smile I could manage, and said, "How can I help you?"

He answered, "I was just waiting here to tell you that you're doing a really good job, Mr. Garlick. Much better than the VP last year."

"Oh! Well, thanks very much! That's good of you to say!" I probably stood up a bit straighter, with a slightly less tired smile.

"You know, you're always telling us, 'Good on you.' Well, I thought it was time for one of us to say the same to you. Good on you, sir. Have a good day, Mr. Garlick."

The Tattoo

One of my jobs as a VP was to interview new kids if they came to the school at a time other than September or January and show them around the building. It didn't happen often, but when kids come mid-semester, they're coming to a new school with different teachers, different kids, and sometimes a few different rules. It's best for them to meet the VP and find out he's not a jerk. Maybe he's somebody they can trust.

Anyway, as I was finishing my interview and tour with one young woman, I noticed she had a tattoo of a naked woman on her shoulder. It looked homemade. It looked like the kind of tattoo a sailor might have had during World War II.

"Ummm . . . I just noticed your tattoo. I don't think it's really appropriate for high school."

"Oh!" she said. "Geesh! Sorry! I forgot all about it. I've had it since I was a kid." (She was sixteen at the time.) "Lemme see . . . Can I borrow a marker?"

I happened to have a red marker in my shirt pocket, so I passed it over to her.

She very carefully drew a bikini onto the tattoo and handed me back the marker.

"There! If I wear a short-sleeved shirt again, I'll be sure to dress the lady better in future. Otherwise, I'll wear long sleeves. Okay?"

The Difference a Couple Letters Can Make

The mother of one of my newer students arrived at the office and asked if she could speak with me in private. I ushered her into my office, closed the door, and sat down at my desk across from her.

She looked very nervous. "I'm not certain how to tell you this, but I need to see my son and maybe take him out of school. I don't know what the protocol is for this sort of thing, and I have no idea what you're going to do about this."

I leaned forward, forearms on my desk. "What's going on? What do you need me to do?"

"I guess I'll just have to tell you. I was cleaning my son's room this morning, after he left for school. I found something that I didn't recognize, so I called my husband on the phone and described it to him. He got very upset and told me it was a pipe bomb."

My heart sank and began to race at the same time. Immediately, I began thinking of all the ramifications, and what I was going to have to do: find out where the boy's locker was, call 9-1-1, empty the building, wait for the police bomb squad to arrive. Call my superintendent. Do I get the kid down here? How best to do that? Should I just call him down? Should I go get him? Alone? With one of my VPs? Is it safe to open the kid's locker? Do I even know the kid is here? I asked myself all these questions within, maybe, two seconds. While I was doing this, the woman continued talking.

"It's clear glass, has a bowl at one end, it's about this long, and he's got stickers on it."

I stopped asking myself questions, turned my full attention back to the woman sitting across from me, felt my heart rate begin to return to normal, and smiled. "Are you sure your husband said it was a pipe bomb?"

"Yes. He asked me if it smelled, and I told him it didn't. He said, well, at least he's not been using it very much then, but he was still pretty angry."

I started giggling and leaned back in my chair.

"I don't see what's so funny, Mr. Garlick."

"I'm sorry. It's just that a pipe *bomb* might explode and kill or injure a number of students and teachers. A pipe *bong*, which you just described, means your son is probably smoking some marijuana. I suppose both are bad, but one's a lot worse. Do you want to speak to your son this evening after school or do you want me to go get him now?"

"Oh . . ."

Why Don't They Like Me?

My first long-term assignment as a supply teacher was for two weeks at a vocational school that's no longer open. To that point, I'd only taught for single days at different schools.

I forget what I was assigned to teach. It was a very long time ago.

I remember, though, being so new and enamoured with the job that even during my spares and lunch, I tried to talk with the kids, in the halls, out front of the building, in the cafeteria.

I was twenty-four, maybe, certainly no more than twenty-five; a fresh-faced kid with what I thought was a pretty cool moustache, but no beard yet.

The first couple days, kids seemed eager to talk with me. Nothing about English or history or whatever I was teaching there; music, food, restaurants, and movies were the topics of choice.

Then on the third day, I noticed that fewer and fewer kids wanted to talk. When I walked down the hall during my spare, kids ducked into class, eager to get away from me. One kid even ducked into a classroom that wasn't his.

I couldn't figure it out and mulled over the conversations I'd had the day before. Had I offended one or more of them? Were my musical tastes *that* different from theirs?

I walked into the office and expressed my disappointment to one of the secretaries, who started to laugh.

"It's not you, David. You're just too young. *Too* close in age to them."

"I don't understand."

"They think you're an undercover police officer. They think you're a narc."

The In-School
Suspension Monitor

No one called her the in-school suspension monitor. The teachers and I called her Linda. The kids called her "miss" or "ma'am." A select few called her the "In-School Suspension Bitch" behind her back. For some reason, none of the kids ever thought to call her by her real name, Mrs. Chakmak. And to be clear, the select few were not being fair.

In-school suspension was not supposed to be pleasant. It was a consequence for poor behaviour or for not getting your work finished. Kids were sent to the room next to my office, to Linda, and Linda enforced the rules.

The rules were simple and easily understood by all, even the select few.

Sit down. Take out your work. Work quietly.

Simple.

Linda brought a small boom box from home and some CDs of her choosing that were meant to add to the consequence of being in the room. Frank Sinatra mostly. If kids were working quietly, the boom box was left off. If Linda had to ask more than a couple times, the CD player was turned on, and she made it clear whose fault it was.

My favourite thing was if a kid made a negative comment about the music.

"Oh. Perhaps you're just not hearing it well. Maybe if I turn it up—"

And then she'd turn it up. When the kids quietened down, as they always did, she let the song end, and then she'd turn it off until the next incident, which usually didn't happen until the next class, or the next day.

Linda was a great in-school suspension monitor.

Only once did a student make a complaint about Linda to me. Well, almost.

I heard "Strangers in the Night" coming from the room next to mine. I smiled. I heard a knock on my door, and a student, one of the select few, came into my office. She sat down across from me and said, "I want to make a complaint about the in-school suspension monitor. Do you know what she just said to me? What she just called me?"

I knew the student was lying, or getting set to. If ever there was an issue that went beyond turning Frank Sinatra up, Mrs. Chakmak would ask me to deal with the student.

I smiled, and before the student could say anything to actually get herself in any real trouble, I said, "You know she's my wife, right?"

"She's your what?"

"She's my wife. Now, what did you say she called you?"

"Oh . . . I'm sorry. I won't do it again."

Linda Chakmak was the best in-school suspension monitor I ever had the pleasure to work with.

A Single Stick of Dynamite

I received a phone call from my old friend, Bill Miller, a little bit ago. When I say "a little bit ago," I mean back when I was vice-principal at Forster. So, around twenty-three years ago. He's called since, but this is the conversation I want to talk about.

Bill and I had worked together at a small program called Directions for students who weren't "buying in" to the regular program. This was far closer to the beginning of my career than its end. We became good friends while working with these kids. After we left Directions, we kind of followed each other around the system, never actually working together again. For example, Bill moved to Massey Secondary, where I had taught previously, and when I went to Forster as vice-principal, Bill had just retired from there.

Anyway, after the normal pleasantries, Bill jumped right into the deep end with this question: "Dave, has anyone mentioned anything to you about a stick of dynamite?"

"*Dynamite?* No. What are you talking about?"

"It's probably gone then."

"Please explain what you're talking about."

"It's just that there used to be a stick of dynamite in the science prep room in the B Wing."

"There was a what? Where?"

"In the B Wing. It was only for display purposes. And I never displayed it. Actually, I never even *saw* it. Just heard about it."

"Bill!"

"It was Clem Anderson's. I don't know where he got it. My *guess* is that it came from a company trying to entice kids into working for them, or maybe it came from the Ministry of Natural Resources. Dynamite is kind of exciting, right? Anyway, it's probably gone."

I don't remember anything else about the conversation. I do remember going into school the next day, a Saturday, and taking a tour of the science prep room in the B wing, by myself, and finding a wooden box about a foot long and six inches wide. I opened it to find, yes, a single stick of dynamite. In fact, the box was labelled:

One (1) stick of dynamite. For display purposes only.

My guess, as opposed to Bill's, was that any teacher who'd found it over the years since Clem Anderson retired just assumed that it was supposed to be there and quickly forgot about it. Or they assumed that it wasn't real and quickly forgot about it. *I* assumed that it *was* real, because

David Garlick

that was my job. I also assumed that it was real because
of all the other stuff I'd found in science prep rooms over
the years: nitro glycerin, for example, in a small glass
bottle stored, alphabetically, next to NaCl (table salt), or
an acid so strong it had begun to turn its glass bottle into
something malleable. I remember picking the bottle up
and feeling my thumb and fingers impress themselves into
the glass. Although I thought that was pretty cool, I also
thought that it wasn't quite right. In fact, it turned out to
necessitate a visit from men in white hazmat suits to take
it away.

I closed the box very carefully and went back to my
office. I quickly did some research on dynamite and
discovered, to my concern, that although dynamite is
relatively stable and safe for, say, the first year or so after
it's created, it doesn't remain so over time. The nitroglyc-
erin in it leeches out of the cardboard tubing and collects
wherever it's stored.

I called my principal right away. And you might not
believe me, but I don't remember which one it was: Elver
Peruzzo or Dave Lynn. Why don't I remember? Because
the conversation was so, well, not what I expected.

"Dynamite?" asked Elver or Dave. "Well, we can't have
that, can we? Leave it with me, okay? Thanks for calling.
Good job. Do me a favour, go back and make sure the
prep room is locked and then email the teachers who use
that room and copy the department head. Tell them that
the room is off limits for Monday."

And that was that. Calm. Matter-of-fact. From the
reaction I received, I might have told him that I'd found

some new graffiti on a bathroom wall. I did as I was directed and ensured the room was locked and that the teachers were notified to stay away for the day on Monday.

And the dynamite disappeared. I know now what must have happened because of similar situations I encountered since. Men in white hazmat suits arrived. Probably on Sunday. Or the police bomb squad arrived; again, probably on Sunday. And they took the dynamite away. Elver or Dave had quiet conversations with the teachers, gently taking them to task for allowing a stick of dynamite to remain in the school for as long as they had, and then told them to go through their inventories and remove anything that was equally dangerous. And the teachers all did.

Was I a part of any of this? No. Do I *know* that this happened as I've just described? Not really. I know Dave and Elver though, and my scenario fits. Elver might have been a bit more emotional than Dave: "*Think* what could have happened! I don't *want* to think what could have happened!" Dave would have described the attitudes of the police officers, along with the damage a stick of dynamite could do to that part of the school.

All I *really* know is that the dynamite disappeared. And it's a measure of the nature of the job that I didn't think to ask about it and that twenty-some-odd years later, I don't remember which of them dealt with it. It's also a measure of the nature of the job that I'm also sure that neither Elver nor Dave would remember the incident unless I remind them of it. I, too, forgot it until I recently watched a short video on YouTube about Alfred Nobel and his invention.

David Garlick

All these years later I'm still impressed by both Dave and Elver and not just because of this situation. They seemed to remain calm and collected in almost every situation. Nothing prepares you for a stick of dynamite in a science lab.

Except for the job of being a principal. The *job* prepares you.

They've Already Won

I have a confession. It won't surprise my friends, but it may surprise a few teachers and students. I'm not much of a sports guy.

I like golf. I'm pretty good at badminton. I used to ski. I own a baseball glove. After I retired, I took up pickleball. I'll watch the occasional baseball or football game on TV. But that's about it.

When I was working though, I always tried to get out and watch a few games of whatever the kids were playing throughout the year. Boys and girls, it didn't make a difference. I'd sit in the stands with the parents, and I'd yell and scream with the best of them. Afterwards, I'd give the kids high fives and "Good on yous." I'd make an announcement the next day. At Lowe Secondary School, I actually coached the badminton team for six years.

So, kids might be surprised to find out that I'm not, really, much of a sports guy.

Despite that, this is one of my favourite stories.

**

"Mr. Garlick? The game will start soon. Remember? You said you trying to watch it this week," said Bujar, smiling at my office door.

Bujar was a tall, thin, dark-haired, dark-eyed student in our school's English Language Learner program. He was sixteen years old. He'd been in Canada for a little less than a year, and like many of the students from Kosovo in our school, he'd struggled on arrival, both to Canada and John L. Forster Secondary School. Initially, he didn't seem to get the idea that he was supposed to be at school five days a week, at the same time each day. He also seemed to enjoy getting in the occasional fight and showing off his newly acquired knowledge of Words You're Not Supposed to Say at School.

He'd been in my vice-principal's office more than a few times, and I'd met both his parents more than once. He'd been sent home a few times, never seeming to mind the consequence when it happened.

Then he found out we had a soccer team.

"Bujar, if you want to play on our team, you have to be at school every day. You can't get into any trouble with me, and I need your teachers to tell me that you're working hard in class."

"But I really good at football, er, soccer. I play, we win."

I leaned forward at my desk and lowered my voice to a whisper. "Let me tell you a secret, Bujar, but you can't tell anyone." I looked to my left and right, making a show of the fact we were alone in my office. I leaned forward even more. "I don't care. I don't care if we win or lose. I don't even care if we have a team. If the players aren't also good students, they won't play and I'll kick them off the team."

Bujar looked shocked, but he saw that I was telling the truth, and he knew that I was a man of my word.

And so Bujar became a good student. Not overnight, but pretty quickly. He made the team, became a leader, and a *true* leader, both on and off the field.

I saw him in the halls telling other players to get to class. I saw him break up an almost-fight before it could get going.

"What's the matter with you! You *want* soccer cancelled? You *want* cut from team? Jesu Cristo, grow up!" I think the "Jesu Cristo" was for my benefit, because Bujar was a Muslim.

When the soccer coach brought me the list of kids who'd made the team, I was surprised to see that I knew most of them. I was the VP, and the kids *I* knew were kids who were in my office often enough for me to know them.

But when I checked through each of their records, I was surprised to find out that, to a kid, they'd not been in any trouble for weeks, had excellent attendance, and their teachers all noted improvement in both effort and marks.

Hmm, I thought. Maybe sports are more important than I give them credit for.

So, when Bujar came to my office after school, of his own volition, not sent by any teacher, to ask me if I'd come to one of their games, I was happy to say "Yes."

"We're good, sir. I think we have chance to be city champions."

"Good on you, Bujar! I'm proud of you! And not only because you've made the team, and the team is good. I'm proud of the leader you've become. And I'm proud of all your teammates! They've all become good students! Thanks!"

Bujar flashed me a winning smile and said, "Our next game is tomorrow. Four o'clock. Across the street. See you then?"

"I wouldn't miss it! See you tomorrow."

The next afternoon, after being reminded by Bujar, I made my way across the street to watch the game. We had no stands next to the field. The parents and kids who came to watch either stood or brought their own folding chairs. Bujar's parents were there. They waved me over, and I stood behind them. I'd missed the first ten minutes of the game, and Forster was behind, one–nil.

Bujar's father's English was better than his son's, and everyone else in his family. "The boys are playing well. They make a good team. They'll get their chances. I think they'll win."

"I don't doubt it," I responded. "Your son's a fine young man, sir. I'm proud to know him."

I forget why, but about ten minutes after I got there, the opposing team called a time out, and our boys raced over to the sidelines to get advice from the coach. I took a good look at the boys who made up the team, and, realizing for the first time exactly what I was witnessing, tears started rolling down my cheeks, caught for a moment by the corners of my smile.

Bujar's father had no way of knowing why I was crying; this silly, smiling man in a suit. He guessed, but he guessed incorrectly.

"No one is hurt, Mr. Garlick. Nothing bad has happened. There's a lot of time. Our boys will win."

The boys were huddled in a circle around the coach, who was on one knee among them. They were listening intently, arms around each other's shoulders. This team of young men, boys really, who were playing so well together, were from Kosovo, Serbia, Bosnia and Herzegovina, Somalia, Ethiopia, and the Sudan. Their home countries were all at war. Some with each other. These boys were all of an age when they would soon be called up for military service, if they were still in their home countries, as enemies, perhaps to try to kill each other.

But here, they were friends, playing soccer as a team, as boys that age should be doing.

I shook my head, as the tears continued to roll down my cheeks. I looked at Bujar's father and smiled, now wiping the tears from my eyes.

"No, sir. You're wrong. Those boys have already won."

Elver and Dave and the Snowstorm

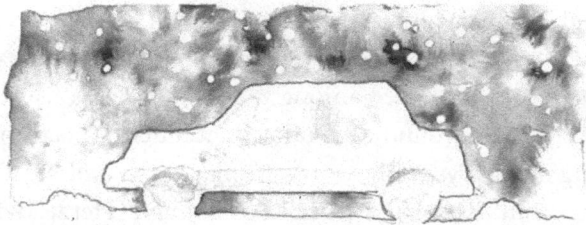

If you know me at all, or have read *The Principal Chronicles*, you already know that I love Elver Peruzzo. I would walk through fire for him. It is because of him that I became a vice-principal in the first place. And yet, we had very different styles of leadership. We had the same basic philosophy though. We both loved kids. We both had great respect for our staffs. And although our styles were very different, they never came into conflict. Part of this was the fact that, as a new vice-principal, self-aware enough to know I didn't know anything at all about the job, that I wasn't any good at it, and grateful to the man for the fact I held the position at all, I always deferred to him.

"Dave, you have to start thinking of the big picture. The whole school. You're not a classroom teacher anymore. You have to stop thinking like one. Big picture."

"But, Elver, I deal with individual kids. One at a time now. Not even a whole class. One."

"Yes, but the *way* you deal with them can affect the whole school. Big picture."

It took me a long time to reconcile those two ways of thinking. I don't know that I ever really did.

But although our styles were different, they were complementary.

I forget why Elver and I needed to drive to school together that day. Perhaps one of his cars needed servicing. In any case, Elver's wife was to drive him to our street, drop him off, and then continue on to her work. This should have worked out fine, but, as the title of the story indicates, this occurred the morning after a terrible snowstorm.

Elver and I had each been out late the night before, shovelling. We were both up early the next day shovelling. But Elver had a garage, so he and his wife didn't have to clean off their car. When he arrived at my house, I'd finished the sidewalk, the porch, and the driveway, and was just beginning to start on my car. The five inches of snow came off easily enough, but revealed the vehicle was encased in hard, almost crystal-clear ice, about a half an inch thick. Try as we might, it would not come away. Elver worked on one side of the car while I worked on the other. The ice was so thick and so hard we couldn't even think about getting a key into the door to unlock it. We chipped and we chipped in silence.

Linda came out to help us. We chipped and we chipped. I'd finally succeeded in creating a small clear patch, about six inches square.

"Do you think my hair dryer might do something?" Linda asked.

"It's worth a try," I replied. "You'll find the long yellow extension cord in the basement."

Linda left to get the hair dryer. I continued chipping. The six-inch square was now a bit larger. Elver suddenly stopped and began walking towards the corner of the street. I continued chipping. I wondered what Elver was doing and, to be honest, was a little upset that he'd just stopped working. If we couldn't get into my car, I had no idea how we were going to get to school on time, and I wondered, What happens if neither the principal nor the vice-principal show up for school?

A couple minutes later, he came back. "There's a snow drift at the corner of the street. You're going to have to gun it to get through and pray that there's no traffic coming on Riverside Drive. I hope the main roads are okay. What do you think we should do if we get to school and find out they haven't plowed out the parking lot?"

Big picture.

I stopped, exhausted. "Elver, why are you worried about the end of this road and a parking lot across the city? I'm still worried that we won't be able to get into my car!"

Little picture.

Elver started chipping again as Linda came out with her hairdryer and the long yellow extension cord.

Complementary.

Added Value or The "Extras"

This is more of an essay than an anecdote or short story. Any names you read will be the real names. Events discussed are exactly as I remember them. For example, Willie Horton of the Detroit Tigers did hit a grand slam in the bottom of the ninth to defeat the Washington Senators, and I was there to watch it, having walked across the Ambassador Bridge with my cub scout pack in 1968 fifty-five years ago. But this piece, really, has very little to do with baseball. Or walking across the bridge, which you're not allowed to do anymore.

It has more to do with the fact that I hate most short forms and acronyms and I'm disappointed that educators have to be held accountable for what they do every day and that principals had to develop SMART goals for SIPSAs in my years as a principal.

Don't misunderstand me. We should be accountable for what we do every day. We should have well-constructed lesson plans and know what we want to teach daily, and have short-term, medium-term, and long-term goals. We should be concerned that our students are successful and leave school being able to do things and know things.

It's just sad, to me, that we have to be able to *prove* it to somebody. And that *that* is what gets all the focus.

The other day, I was going through some of my notebooks from when I was a principal. I kept a notebook on my desk or in my hand every day for seventeen years. Phone numbers, notes taken after a student fight, complaints from parents, notes from meetings, rough notes from teacher evaluations, investigations, ideas—that kind of thing. As I read through them, whenever I came to a principals' meeting, I may as well have written, "Blah, blah, blah," for seven or eight pages. Acronyms that, at the time, meant something to me, I guess. SIPSA, for example, stood for School Improvement Plan for Student Achievement. It was meant to be an improvement from SIP (School Improvement Plan), and it had to be prepared every year using the board's template and state which goals we'd established each year for our students to achieve, what percentage would pass the OSSLT (Ontario Secondary School Literacy Test), how many would pass all four of their classes each semester, and what we were going to *do* to achieve those goals each year.

To be honest, and I remember saying this out loud at a principals' meeting, these things offended me as a teacher and principal.

"Offended?! What can you find offensive about wanting kids to be successful each year?" asked Mr. or Ms. Superintendent, incredulous, and secretly upset at the comment and being interrupted.

"I find it offensive that in September or October of every year, my committee and I have to sit down and establish a reasonable and achievable goal that, say, just for argument's sake, 85 percent of our kids will pass the OSSLT, which also means we're setting, as a *goal,* that 15 percent will fail."

"Dave, you're *allowed* to do better than your goal."

They didn't understand.

Good teachers and principals are idealists. Every September, they *know* that this year will be the year that every student will love their classes, and everyone will be there every day, and everyone will pass and do better than they expected. If you're a principal, it will be the year of no fights, no suspensions, and no complaints. And there will be more than enough money in the budget for all the activities everyone wants to do, and the photocopier will never break down.

But we're also realists. We look at our class lists and think, Oh, *that* kid again.

And our room will be too hot or too cold. Or we won't even have a room of our own. Or we have to share our room with *that* teacher, who always leaves his coffee cup on my pile of marking. And the principal won't appreciate all the *extra* stuff I do. And 15 percent is probably a reasonable guess of how many kids will fail.

It's depressing to acknowledge that one month into the school year. And we shouldn't have to. Because, in the end, it might not be that important.

Here's what I mean. I was always one of the *value-added* teachers. I taught my three seventy-five-minute classes a day, but in addition to that, I was the liaison to student parliament, the badminton coach, the organizer of the annual trip to Stratford, the organizer of the annual food drive, and I was the organizer of Buddy Week (sort of a Secret Santa thing in February for staff). I'm not saying any of this to brag. There were lots of teachers like me on staff. Most of us did these sorts of things. Some did a lot more. As I reflect, I think that for a lot of kids, those things were far more important than anything they learned, or didn't learn, in class.

That extra stuff—the value-added stuff—that *kept* a lot of students in school: it gave them a reason to come each day, and then learn their math and science and English and history, and then eventually graduate and go on to college, or university, or work.

And when I think back to *my* time in school, even though I was successful and liked my time there enough to want to spend thirty-three years actually working in high schools, I have a hard time remembering any lessons I learned in school. That's also true for elementary school.

What *do* I remember? I remember walking across the Ambassador Bridge to watch the Tigers play the Washington Senators and seeing Willie Horton hit a grand slam to win the game. I remember a train trip to London's Storybook Gardens in Grade 1 with Miss Onika; being part of a mass choir on the stage of the Cleary Auditorium, singing "Yellow Bird"; a few show-and-tells but, interestingly, not my part in them; playing in a jazz band on the stage of the Top Hat Lounge, and getting a free lunch for it! All that was before I even started high school.

In high school, it was the band and concerts. Acting in plays. A trip to Stratford, my first, to see *Love's Labour's*

Lost. Band trips to Montreal, Ottawa, Erie, Pennsylvania, and Perth. Getting smacked by an old woman during intermission who said, "You should be *nicer* to your sister!" I was playing Helen Keller's older brother James in *The Miracle Worker*, and I guess I did an okay job of it.

I was never going to be a professional musician or actor. I was an avid reader. I *suggested* to the teacher working in the library, Donna Lanktree, that she buy a copy of *Do Black Patent Leather Shoes Really Reflect Up?* and she did!

And then, in passing, she said, "You know, David, I think you may be almost as well read as I am!"

That would have been sometime in 1977—forty-six years ago, as I write this. I had been thinking then of maybe someday being a teacher. Donna's comment, outside of class, made in passing to a *good* but not outstanding student, cemented that for me.

The work in class is important. But it's the value-added stuff that makes an education complete.

Lunchtime Moments at Western Secondary

Hidden Talents

In late September one year, I was talking with a group of four Grade 9 students in the cafeteria. They were new to the school, still finding out where they fit in. I happened to know that the four of them came from different schools and would not have known each other before arriving at Western. In less than a month, they'd found each other and become friends. (In fact, they remained friends for the entire time they were at high school. Not bad for four kids with at least one, but probably several, learning disabilities.)

"Hey! Mr. Garlick! Come here! Look what Carlie can do!"

I sat down with the group.

"Watch this!"

I looked at Carlie, a fourteen-year-old blonde girl, who smiled at me, closed her eyes, and then wiggled her nose, just like Samantha in *Bewitched*. The four of them thought this was hilarious. But before they'd stopped laughing, Carlie said, "That's nothing! Watch Jamie!"

Jamie was a young boy with a cleft palate. In a lot of schools, Jamie would have been the victim of at least a bit of taunting or bullying because of it, but, so far as I knew, it wasn't even mentioned by any of the kids in Grade 9, or at any point in his high school career.

We looked at Jamie, who smiled, stared at me, and then waggled both his ears, back and forth. We all laughed, and then Jamie said, "I'm working on wiggling each of them separately, but it's pretty hard. I'll get it by the end of the semester though."

One of the other kids said, "If you can't, that's okay. I can't wiggle my nose or my ears at all! I'll bet you didn't know you had such talented kids, did you, sir?"

"That's the thing. I know I've got hundreds of talented kids here. I just don't know, yet, what those talents are. And very often, neither do they."

Respect Can Look Different to Different People

Lunchtime supervision is different for a principal—different from what a teacher experiences. Some teachers seem to view it as though they're prison guards. They're missing the uniform and the billy club or taser, but apart from that, they look like "screws" in a penitentiary.

Some others see it as something that *has* to be done each month. "I've got to do cafeteria supervision this week. That's a half hour each day I'll never get back."

Others see it as a time to connect with the kids outside of class. These are the teachers most like I was. They recognize that kids act differently in the cafeteria than they do in class, and supervision is a chance to show the kids that they aren't just an auto teacher, or a math teacher. They are also a human being.

For a principal, though, in some ways, it's actually a break in the schedule. In some ways, it's also the most important part of their day.

At Western, I looked forward to lunchtime supervision. Although I think I was generally liked by most kids, I was given a measure of respect some teachers weren't. If they saw that I was in the cafeteria, they usually wouldn't act up, not out of fear of consequences, but because, in the main, they didn't want to cause me any extra work during *lunch* of all times. I knew this because of the nature of the conversations I had with senior kids. They didn't change the their *talk* at all with me. The occasional "bad word" would creep in, and no one would notice. I tried hard not to notice. Some might see this as disrespectful of the kids, but I saw it as incredibly respectful. They saw me as someone they could talk with, someone who wouldn't stop them when they got carried away with a story, and someone who would answer questions honestly, like they would with me.

"Mr. Garlick, did you have anything to do with hiring Miss X?"

I'd been talking with a group of four senior boys. (I hired a number of new teachers, sometimes three or four a year. We needed new science teachers, math teachers, and English teachers; not every year, and not for every subject, but new teachers nonetheless and, typically, they were young.)

Just as the question was asked, Miss X walked by. She was young and, yes, she was also very attractive. I answered honestly, "Yes, I did. We needed a new teacher of _____." (Fill in the blank with the subject of your choice.)

They let her pass, being quiet and respectful. When she was three or four steps past us, they looked at me, and in one voice, the four of them said, "Thank you, Mr. Garlick."

What's New, Shane?

By the middle of October, I'd noticed that Shane often sat by himself at lunch. I didn't know if this was by choice or if he hadn't found a group of friends yet.

"Hey, Shane! How's it going? What's new?"

"Hi, Mr. Garlick! Things are going pretty well, thanks. Nothing much is new, I guess."

"Mind if I join you for a bit? If you'd rather I not, that's okay. Some people don't like the principal sitting with them."

"No, it's okay. Please, have a seat."

I sat down across from him. "So. Your classes okay? No issues?"

"Nope. Everything's fine." Then after a couple seconds, a big smile broke across his face. "I thought of something new!"

"What's that, Shane?"

"Girls!"

I laughed. "Girls are hardly *new,* Shane."

"They are to me!" Shane leaned forward, conspiratorially, looking left then right, about to share a secret. "You know, Mr. Garlick, there are an awful lot of really pretty girls here. I mean, just look at Nancy over there!"

I looked over at Nancy. "You're right, Shane. Nancy is a very pretty girl."

Shane looked shocked at my agreement. "You shouldn't talk that way, Mr. Garlick! You're married!"

"Shane, I'm married, but I'm still allowed to find people attractive."

"Oh . . . I guess . . . Say, do you think you could get me her phone number?"

I chuckled. "So, I'm not supposed to find girls attractive, but it'd be okay for me to go over there and ask for her phone number?"

"Well, when you put it like that, maybe not."

The Lost Weekend(s)

"You know, I just realized, for some reason, I haven't written anything about Pumpkinfest yet," I said to my wife while sitting at the computer.

"Well, except for the fact that you always called it the Lost Weekend, what can you write about Pumpkinfest?" Linda asked me. "You were up before 5:00 on Saturday and Sunday and drove home in the dark. Anything else?"

I smiled. "Well, there was the man who trapped himself in the boys' bathroom."

"What, do you mean in one of the stalls?"

"Yup. And there was the time we had to call an ambulance."

"I'd forgotten about that."

"You can't have forgotten the bouncy castle and the bouncy slide."

"I *had* forgotten. You should write something about Pumpkinfest."

I loved Pumpkinfest. It was the best weekend each year at Western Secondary School. In some ways, it was even better than graduation, because I got the same positive feelings about the school, felt the same pride, and received just as many compliments from everyone that spoke to me, but I didn't have to say good-bye to any great kids.

Pumpkinfest was the school's major fundraiser each year, just before Hallowe'en. It was the largest free craft show in the county, and we had repeat exhibitors from across the province and as far away as Nova Scotia. Each of them paid us $50 to rent a table and two chairs, so before the weekend even began, we'd made more than $10,000.

Some staff and students stuck around on the Friday before the event to turn what had been a vibrant high school into the largest crafters' mall in Essex County, maybe in the whole province. Tables and chairs were set up throughout the halls, the cafeteria, several of the larger classrooms, and the gymnasium. Blue plastic matting had to be put down over the gym floor so all the foot traffic and tables wouldn't damage it. The classrooms had to be secured and emptied so that teacher resources and student work didn't go missing. And after everything was over, on the Sunday, we had to turn the crafters' mall back into a high school.

It was a lot of work.

When we left on the Friday evening, it was already "county dark" outside. A dark so complete that, except for the occasional streetlight or farm light, it felt heavy on your face as you drove home.

I usually got home that Friday sometime after 8:30. I'd eat a late dinner, get to bed, and be up the next morning before 5:00 so I could get to school to turn on the all the lights and then open the doors for the vendors, who would be outside waiting at 6:00.

Turning on the lights wasn't as easy as you might think. First, I had to remember where all the switches were—at first in almost complete darkness—with a light switch "key. This key was a small piece of forked metal. I had to insert it into the light switch and then toggle it up or down. I became pretty adept at it, but it was not easy.

Sam Thomas, the wonderful young teacher who ran Pumpkinfest every year, loved the event, and worked throughout the year to ensure its success, was either waiting for me when I got there or the first in line when I went to open the doors at 7:00.

"Good morning, Dave!" she'd say, with a smile on her face. "Are we ready for this?"

We were.

Kids and teachers all arrived long before the doors opened to the public, happy to volunteer their time. Our outside property was turned into a huge parking lot, kids and teachers acting as attendants in bright orange vests, directing cars and trucks this way and that. A small table was set up at the door, not for admission, but to welcome visitors, answer questions, and ask, politely, for donations.

Hundreds of dollars came into the school this way. Our hospitality department prepared all kinds of food, both for the Saturday and Sunday lunch at the school and also to take home after your visit was finished. They made the best meat pies in the world. The breads and cakes and pies and doughnuts, well, they were *out* of this world. Some of our classes set up shop as vendors too.

Once we opened the doors to the public, a steady stream of visitors arrived, literally thousands of people over the two days. But although I've always referred to it as "the Lost Weekend," the reality was that after I opened the doors, my main job for the next two days was just to accept the thanks of the vendors and the kudos of the public. "Your kids are amazing! So polite and helpful!" "The food is fantastic!" "How is it possible for the bread and those meat pies to be so reasonably priced?" "We wait all year for this event!" "A lot of our Christmas shopping gets done here!" "I don't know what we'd do if there wasn't a Pumpkinfest!"

I'd smile and thank people, shaking their hands and accepting pats on the back. That was my job.

Unless there were issues.

I was sitting in the office, preparing to make any announcements Sam Thomas wanted me to make: "Lunch will start at 11:00 today! Try our new tortilla bowl salad! Thanks for coming everyone and we hope you have a great day!" This was *not* a tough assignment. But then, over the walkie-talkie: "Dave, you're needed outside by the bouncy slide! A mother and her daughter are crying!" Just as Sam finished that sentence, I heard a child scream.

I tried to get to the bouncy slide and castle as quickly as I could, but there were maybe a thousand people in my way. I felt like a salmon swimming upstream. Many people wanted to thank me, or congratulate me, or tell me what great kids I had, and I didn't want anyone to think that there might be a *very* serious incident waiting for me outside the school. Worst-case scenarios were things I always had to consider, and I knew there were many that would make a mother cry and a child scream, broken bones among them.

I finally got to the bouncy castle and found a mother, holding her crying daughter by the hand, and the bouncy castle vendor raising his voice in frustration.

"Lady, look, I keep telling ya, if you want the kid to go in the bouncy castle, it's gonna cost you two bucks, okay?"

"But I keep telling you, I've already paid two dollars for the slide, and my daughter didn't even go down it! She got to the top and was too frightened to slide down. Can't she just go in the castle instead?"

"Lady, the slide's not mine! I keep tellin' ya! I got nothin' for the two bucks you gave Joey!"

This discussion had been going on for at least five minutes, and neither side was going to budge. I reached into my pocket and pulled out a toonie. Both the vendor and the woman said, at the same time, "Mr. Garlick! You shouldn't have to pay!"

I picked the little girl up and placed her in the bouncy castle. "As long as the girl is happy."

Then, again over the walkie-talkie: "Mr. Garlick, you're needed at the boys' bathroom. There's a man trapped in one of the stalls."

I could not figure out how this was a possibility. The stalls all had a simple sliding latch, like millions of public bathrooms around the world. I was met outside the bathroom by one of my senior students. "He says he's trapped, sir. He sounds pretty calm, but he says he can't get out."

I walked into the bathroom and said, "Hi, sir! I'm David Garlick. I'm the principal of the school. We're going to get you out of there, okay?"

"I'm trapped." He did sound pretty calm.

"Sir? Do you see the latch? Slide it as far as you can to the left, okay?"

I heard the latch move.

"Okay. Good. Now push the door towards me."

"*Towards* you?"

"Yes, sir."

The door swung open, revealing a rather sheepish looking man.

"Geez, I must've been pulling the whole time. Thanks. I was trapped."

Once, I had to call an ambulance. Again, over the walkie-talkie: "Dave? I think you should call an ambulance. An elderly woman fainted in the bathroom and was completely unresponsive for at least two or three minutes. She's come around, but she sounds awfully confused. I've sent a student to get a cool bottle of water."

When I thought of all of the things that might cause a woman to lose consciousness and be confused, I knew

I had to call 9-1-1. I then began the process, over the walkie-talkie, of getting the school's driveway cleared, with students and staff in place to direct the ambulance to the closest door. This was no small feat, with more than a thousand people in the school, hundreds of cars in the parking lot, and more coming in and leaving all the time.

But by the time I made it to the parking lot, they'd cleared just about everyone away, except for one car. "I'm waiting for my wife. She should be out in just a minute, okay?"

"Sir, I'm sorry. You're going to have to move your car. There's an ambulance on the way, and it's going to need to be right where you are now!" As I said all this, I heard the siren of the ambulance, and it sounded to be only a couple city blocks away.

"An ambulance! What did you call an ambulance for?"

"Sir! I need you to move your car NOW! A woman has lost consciousness, and we need to get her to the hospital! Please! Move your car now!"

"That sounds pretty serious. Okay. Say, do you think maybe the lady is my wife?

I saw the ambulance enter our driveway.

"That seems pretty unlikely, don't you think? There's maybe two thousand people in the school. Please just move!"

The car moved out of the way just as the ambulance pulled up. Two students guided the attendants to the bathroom. I tried to get to the bathroom as quickly as I could, but just as with the bouncy slide and castle, people felt they had to stop me to tell me what responsible and polite students I had, that they hoped the lady would be okay, and what did I think was wrong with her? Had her children been notified? One man stopped me to tell me he was qualified in first aid and CPR if they needed him.

"I'm sure that won't be necessary, but thanks."

"One never knows, sir. Let them know, okay?"

By the time I was able to get to the bathroom, the old lady was sitting up, being looked at by the two attendants, her husband holding her hand.

"But I feel fine! Once that nice girl brought me a bottle of water I felt right as rain! I don't want to go to the hospital. I want to stay here."

"We think you should get checked out at the hospital. We don't know why you passed out. Maybe it was nothing, but maybe it was something that needs to be dealt with."

"I guess . . . We can always come back tomorrow, right, honey?"

"Sure, Martha. I'll follow the ambulance to the hospital."

I looked at the old man for the first time since I walked into the bathroom. He looked at me and smiled. "Whaddaya know? It *was* my wife! What are the chances? Thanks for being so persistent and getting me out of the way of the ambulance!"

That might seem like a contrived statement, something I might have made up to write this story. But it's not, and neither were any of the compliments that people gave my students over the years.

Pumpkinfest was always an amazing, though lost, weekend for me.

Jesus St. John

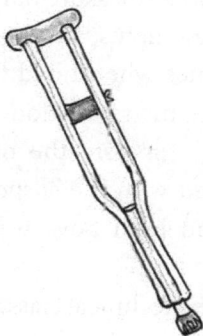

He was tough, maybe the toughest kid I ever worked with. How tough was he? His name was Jesus St. John. I'm not making this up. Jesus St. John. Can you think of a more religious-sounding name? It's important that you know it was pronounced "Hay-zeus," though, and everybody called him either Hay-zeus or Zeus. I always called him Zeus.

No one called him Jesus.

Well, maybe on the first day of school. A teacher or two, who didn't know him, might make that mistake. No one would laugh. He'd correct them politely and ask, again politely, that he either be called Zeus or Hay-zeus.

It's a measure of his toughness—not the only measure—that nobody ever called him Jesus St. John, though I'm sure many were tempted.

Anyway, he was tough. His father and all his brothers were gang members, or former gang members, and had all been in trouble with the police. But not Zeus. At sixteen, I thought this was another measure of his toughness.

He'd been in a few fights, not many. His father had to come to school once when I had to suspend Zeus for one of them. Despite his reputation, and the fact that I was "consequencing" his son, the man was polite and respectful, and agreed with the suspension. He saw that I was being fair, and both boys were being given the same consequence.

Zeus excelled in the technical classes we offered; woodworking, welding, and auto shop were his favourites. This story starts out in his Grade 11 auto shop class.

By Grade 11, our kids were able to work on their own cars, or their parents' cars, changing the oil, rotating and balancing the tires, that kind of thing. Parents all liked this, because oil changes were done at cost. That meant if you supplied the oil, the change was free, although donations to the program were always appreciated. Kids liked it because it meant they got to show off their cars and actually drive them a bit during class, to bring them into the shop.

One of the kids, it's not really important who he was, but let's call him Tom, was backing his father's van into the shop, and Zeus was directing him from behind. The kid, like Zeus, was sixteen. He was using the rear-view mirror and the side-view mirror watching Zeus waving his arms, indicating, "Back, back, back, keep coming."

Something caused Tom to lose focus, so he didn't see Zeus make the sign for, "Okay, you're good. You can stop now." He also didn't see Zeus make the sign for, and then shout, "Stop already! I'm right behind the van! If you don't stop, you're going to—"

Pin Zeus's leg between the van and a filing cabinet.

He was going very slowly, and so Zeus wasn't seriously hurt. He was pinned though, and it did hurt. So when he grunted and threatened to beat the heck out of the kid at the wheel, the kid at the wheel threw the van into park, leapt from the van, and took off, leaving Zeus pinned and the van running.

Fortunately, the teacher was Johnny-on-the-Spot and jumped into the van to pull it forward.

Zeus limped around the shop for a few seconds and then turned to leave.

"Where are you going, Jesus?" asked the teacher.

"I'm going to walk this off, and then I'm going to find that kid and beat the heck out of him. Jerk." (I've always chosen to believe Zeus was referring to the kid and not the teacher.)

While all this was going on, I was in my office, blissfully unaware that any of this was happening. I looked up from my desk to see the kid who'd been at the wheel of the van race by my office.

My secretary, Dorothy, said, "That can't be good. Tom looked pretty scared."

Just then, the auto shop teacher called into the office to tell us what happened and that Zeus was *really* angry.

All these years later, maybe ten or more, I don't know how I did it, but I can still see it happening. I got up from my desk as quickly as I could and placed my right foot in front of my left foot and then, for some reason, tried to bring my left foot forward, but from behind and *to the right* of my right foot. As I said, I can still see my feet doing this, and as I fell forward, I remember thinking how stupid that was, and that it was really going to hurt when I drove both knees into the floor.

I felt a white flash of pain and was surprised when I was able to stand up only a couple of seconds later. I limped out into the hall, just as Zeus came limping by.

When he saw me, he felt certain that I was making fun of him, and his anger became directed at me.

"It's not funny, sir! I'm in real pain here!"

"I am too, Zeus! Stop for a minute, would you?"

When Zeus saw that I too was really in pain, his anger evaporated. "Are you okay, sir? Geez, what happened?"

"I tripped over my feet trying to get out here to stop you from beating the heck out of Tom. Are you okay, Zeus?"

Zeus limped over to me to help me back into the office. We both started laughing as I opened the door, and Dorothy said, "You two look like the walking wounded!"

We collapsed into the chairs that were normally reserved for kids waiting to see me, both of us laughing. And then, at the same time, we said, "Are you going to be okay?" We laughed some more.

"Are you still planning to beat the heck out of Tom?"

"Nah. You can't stay angry if you're having a good laugh, can you? You saved Tom from a good beating though, sir. And you probably saved me from a suspension. Thanks."

As we sat there laughing, I thought that the laughter, the thanks from Zeus, and the story I'd just earned were well worth the momentary pain my feet had caused me.

Emma Bridgewater and the Irish Republican Army

Emma Bridgewater is an English designer, famous for her pottery. Some people are surprised to find out that she really exists, but she does. The Irish Republican Army (IRA) is, well, the Irish Republican Army, and I don't know if it still exists. So far as I know, they have absolutely nothing to do with Emma Bridgewater.

In the summer of 2013, I went to England on a principal exchange. My wife and I stayed with a wonderful head-master and his wife: Steve Colledge and his teacher-wife Anna. Before we went, I'd never heard of the town of Cirencester or the village of Moreton-in-Marsh, but now, they're two of my favourite places on Earth. Steve and

Anna continue to be good friends. And we've been back to visit them since.

I'd been to England twice before the exchange, but this was the first time since I became a principal. And so, this would also be the first time I would receive a call from one of the administrative assistants at the board office before leaving.

"Dave, you're leaving for England in a couple weeks, right?" asked Lynne Higginbottom.

"Yes, ma'am, really looking forward to it, too."

"Could I ask you to do a small favour for me?"

"Sure! What can I do?"

"I broke the lid of my favourite tea pot. It's an Emma Bridgewater." She said that as though she expected the name to mean something to me, and when I mentioned it to my wife later that evening, it was clear that they both thought so. "They're happy to replace it for me, but the cost to ship it to Canada makes it prohibitive. It would cost more than the whole tea pot cost me originally."

"So what would you like me to do?"

"It would be free if it were shipped within the UK, so if I had it shipped under your name to the place you're staying, it would be free. Could you take delivery of it and bring it home for me?"

"That sounds simple enough. Sure. Happy to."

And then I continued to prepare for my trip. I'd been exchanging emails with Steve Colledge for a couple months by this time, and so I asked him if I could use his mailing address for a single piece of mail. I told him it was for an Emma Bridgewater teapot lid, saying it as though I expected him to understand what that meant. I packed. I found as many Ontario and Canada trinkets as I could, assured that English students would find the Canadian flag pins fascinating (they did), and they would think the Canada pens, keychains, and lanyards were as cool as I thought they were (I *think* they did). I was to be spending two weeks at Steve's school and then a week in Moreton-in-Marsh on holiday, because the English school year is a bit different than the Ontario school year.

I studied the itineraries: the one of the entire experience and the places we'd go as a team, and the one of the flight over. Because we came from all over Canada, there was no way we could all fly over on the same plane, but we were all expected to meet at the same time in one particular terminal at Heathrow Airport, no matter where or when our flights landed, and then we'd all board the same buses and head out to Gloucester.

I didn't *really* understand how that was supposed to work. But I had faith that it would.

Because school was already out in Ontario when we left, I didn't have to worry about anything going wrong at my school while I was gone. My wife and I made the same arrangements we always made with the neighbours, and they made with us: to take in the mail, water the plants, and cut the lawn once.

Lynne Higginbottom only called me once to remind me about the Emma Bridgewater teapot lid. I confirmed for her the address I was staying at, the date I was leaving, and the date I was coming home.

"Thanks a lot, David. I love that teapot!"

Finally, departure day arrived, and we left. We flew to Toronto and met up with *some* of the people who would be taking part in the exchange, but again, had faith we'd meet up with the rest in London. But it didn't happen that way. We met up with *some* of the people we were supposed to meet in London. About half. We waited and we talked.

And then we grew concerned.

We grew concerned, because it began to look like we would have to figure out how to get to Gloucester on our own, and then we'd have to figure out where in Gloucester we were supposed to be. And then someone thought to call one of the members of our group who *wasn't* there, on the chance that they were somewhere else at Heathrow, which turned out to be the case.

Half of us were where we were supposed to be, and half of us were where we were supposed to be but in a different place. The signage at Heathrow was to blame. The bus arrived shortly after that, and we all ended up in Gloucester at the same time. My faith was justified. Sort of.

Steve Colledge was waiting for us there. He loaded our luggage into his car and off we sped to the town of Cirencester, where we'd spend the next two weeks. His wife Anna had prepared the first of many tremendous meals, and following that, we sat down in the living room to trade stories, laugh, and play with their several cats.

I forget how my name came up, and why so much time had gone by without mentioning it. It probably had something to do with Garlick Heath in London, and how I'd found it on my first trip to England in 1985.

"Here . . . What did you say your name is?" asked Anna. I thought maybe she knew some other Garlicks. It's a more common name than you might think.

"Dave. Dave Garlick."

She turned to Steve, suddenly very serious. "You didn't tell me a Dave Garlick was staying with us!" I was a bit concerned. I didn't know what I could have done for my name to cause such a change in the mood.

"I think I must have," said Steve. "He's going to be staying with us for two weeks and we've been emailing back and forth for a bit."

"No. You never told me."

"Well, you know now."

She turned back to me. "A piece of mail arrived for you this morning."

"Oh! Yes! It's a tea pot lid! I promised a friend I'd bring it back to Canada for her! It's an Emma Bridgewater."

"It's gone," she said. "I'd never heard of David Garlick, so when the postman said it was for a David Garlick, I told them that I didn't know a David Garlick and refused to accept it!"

"Oh . . . Well in Canada, it would just go back to the post office. So tomorrow, I'll call and have them deliver it here again."

"That's not what happens in Britain," said Anna.

When I looked at Steve, I saw that he had closed his eyes and was pinching the top of his nose, as though he had a bad headache.

"What happens in Britain?" Linda asked.

"Well, because of the troubles with the Irish Republican Army and mail bombs in the 1970s, we're instructed not to take mail that's not intended for us, or that we're not expecting. All such mail is sent to Northern Ireland and exploded there."

"Exploded?"

"Yes. Ka-boom."

"Oh . . ."

"If it was just this morning, maybe it hasn't gone to be exploded yet," said Steve, sounding almost upbeat about things. "Maybe, if we call first thing in the morning, it won't get blown up."

"And, worst-case scenario, if it does get blown up, I've got three weeks to order another one. Not to worry."

"I can't believe you didn't tell me David's last name!"

And that's where we ended things that evening. Steve was suitably chastened for not telling Anna my name, Anna was concerned about the fate of the Emma Bridgewater teapot lid, and I had learned that Brits were still so concerned about the IRA sending them mail bombs that unopened packages were still being blown up on a regular basis.

Steve called the post office the next morning before we sat down to breakfast. Whoever he spoke to was reasonably sure that the Emma Bridgewater teapot lid had yet to be exploded, though he couldn't be certain.

"If we find the package for David Garlick, we won't send it off to be blown up" is what I think Steve was told.

And then Steve and I left for school. Anna and Linda left for downtown Cirencester about an hour after us, and just as they were turning on to the street that would lead them to the downtown, they were passed by a Royal Mail truck going in the opposite direction and heading into their subdivision.

"You don't suppose . . ." said Linda to Anna.

"There are lots of Royal Mail trucks. That one *probably* isn't going to our house."

"I suppose, but what happens if there's no one there when the truck *does* deliver it?"

"Steve didn't say."

Anna turned around and drove back to their house. They arrived, just in time to see the truck, *a* truck, turning left at the end of their block, having presumably already been to their house.

"Shoot! Should I make off after it? Chase it down?"

"Maybe they placed the teapot lid in your mailbox."

"Good point."

Anna pulled into her driveway and, as quickly as she could, ran to her mailbox.

"There's nothing here! Maybe if we hurry, we can catch the truck!"

Again, as quickly as she could, she dashed back to the car and threw it into reverse.

"This is exciting, isn't it? Kind of like a James Bond chase scene!" she said, as she finished backing into the street, putting the car in drive. "I read recently Royal Mail trucks turn left whenever they can. Saves on petrol and time. Fewer accidents as well."

"Well please be careful. *We* don't need to get into an accident for this. It's just a teapot lid," said Linda.

And so, the two middle-aged ladies chased a Royal Mail truck through the streets of Cirencester, never really coming close to catching up with it but sometimes seeing it as it usually turned left at the end of the street they'd just entered.

"Oh no! It's headed for the M-way!" Anna shouted.

Linda had only been in England for just over twenty-four hours at this point, and so wasn't entirely sure what this meant, but knew that it didn't sound good.

"That's not good, is it?" she sought to confirm.

"Not at all! Because that also means it's headed for the Magic Roundabout, and if it gets there we're lost!"

For Canadian readers: an M-way, short for motor-way, is similar to our 400-series highways. The Magic Roundabout is similar to, well, nothing at all in the Canadian experience.

"What's the Magic Roundabout?" Linda asked.

"You're about to find out, dearie!"

The Magic Roundabout is a series of five roundabouts that ring a central and far larger roundabout, and before you ask, yes, it is actually called the Magic Roundabout. Once you're in it, you can aim your automobile towards virtually anywhere in the United Kingdom, hence "magic," but it is incredibly confusing to use as you can end up heading toward anywhere in the UK.

Anna handled it very well, from the standpoint of not getting lost, and not getting into a car accident, and, eventually, getting her car pointed back towards Cirencester, but not from the standpoint of catching a Royal Mail truck. In fact, once they got into the Magic Roundabout,

Linda counted four different Royal Mail trucks all headed to different parts of the country.

"I think we need to give up and go have a cup of tea and a scone in Cirencester," Anna said.

"That sounds like a very good plan to me," agreed Linda.

And so, their James Bond episode came to an end, and they enjoyed a very nice cup of tea and a scone together, getting to know one another.

"We've got three weeks here in England," Linda reasoned. "That's more than enough time to order another teapot lid and have it shipped to your house. You drive very well, by the way. James Bond would be proud."

After their tea and scone, and a walk around the downtown, they drove back home. Anna checked their mailbox before unlocking the front door and was disappointed, but not surprised, to find no package addressed to David Garlick. She and Linda went in and sat down to another cup of tea.

They chatted about Canada, Linda's career as an archivist, Anna's career as a French teacher, Steve and Anna's adult children, and the family's many pets. And then the doorbell rang. It was Simon from next door.

"Hi, Anna," he said. "This package isn't for you. It's for the Canadian principal who's coming to stay with you. Steve asked me to accept any mail that might come for a David Garlick if you two weren't here. This arrived this morning. Please, give it to him when he gets here."

"When did Steve tell you about David Garlick?" Anna asked.

"Oh, weeks and weeks ago! Maybe a month. But he only told me about the mail a couple weeks ago. Told me it was a teapot lid."

"Did he?" she asked through almost gritted teeth.

Anna accepted the package and thanked Simon. She did *not* slam the door.

"That man! Steve thinks to tell Simon, the next-door neighbour, about a David Garlick and a package of mail, but not his own wife! What am I going to do with him?"

"Dave's the same," Linda sympathized. "His head is so full of stuff—of school and kids, and parents, and meetings, that he'll often forget to tell me things like he won't be home for dinner or he has to be at school for five in the morning. It's maddening!"

Over the next couple hours, Anna and Linda commiserated and found out how much their marriages had in common, and they began to find the entire Emma Bridgewater–James Bond–Irish Republican Army–teapot episode humourous.

"It'd be funny if David opened it, and it was broken, wouldn't it?" Anna asked.

"Knowing Dave, he'll find a way to break it *as* he's giving it to Lynne!"

"Really?"

"No, but it wouldn't be a complete surprise. Dave's a klutz."

Steve and I arrived home that evening at the normal time that Steve would arrive home after a day of school.

"Linda and I spent half the day chasing down a Royal Mail carrier to rescue the Emma Bridgwater teapot lid!

Here it is!" Anna announced as we walked in the door. "Because of that, I haven't had time to put anything on for dinner. So, you get to go to the Chinese restaurant for fish and chips. Don't forget the coleslaw this time!"

As you've probably guessed, Anna and Linda told us the true story over our fish and chips, which were excellent. It turns out that the Chinese restaurant in Cirencester also makes the best fish and chips in town. They told the story in turns, like a seasoned pair of sports announcers.

"And then we entered the Magic Roundabout!"

"Dave, we're lucky to be alive!"

We laughed a lot that evening, as we did most every evening that trip. Anna was referred to as Anna Bond and Anna Andretti several times throughout the trip.

As has so often happened to me, and I'm guessing with Steve as well, what started out as something that exasperated my wife turned into something that made both of us laugh for months or years afterward. We're both lucky that way.

I packed the teapot lid away in my luggage and didn't look at it again until I unpacked everything back in Windsor, although more than a few times on that trip, Linda would point out Emma Bridgwater designs to me when we saw them in different shops throughout England.

After recovering from jet lag, I went to the school board to give Lynne Higginbottom her teapot lid.

"Thanks so much, David" a very grateful Lynne exclaimed when I gave it to her. "I hope it didn't cause you any trouble."

"Me? No. No trouble at all."

They're Not Real People!

In teachers' college, I trained to be a secondary school teacher. All the courses I took, and all my practice teaching, was aimed at becoming a teacher of secondary school-aged students. This was the case for all the teacher candidates in my classes as well.

We often made fun of those who were training to be elementary school teachers. They always sounded overly chipper and walked with a spring in their step that somehow seemed contrived. When they said "Good morning!" it was always in a sing-song manner. This seemed to be especially true on the mornings after we'd been out over-late, *not* studying, and were dealing with headaches or hangovers.

Now, having written all of that, the *reality* was that we were actually training to teach students from Grades 7 and up. Grade 7. That meant that any of us could have ended up working in elementary school. And 1983 was not a year of big hiring in the province, so another reality was that none of us training to be teachers of English and history could afford to be choosy. If we were lucky, we might catch on as occasional teachers. A small number of us got actual classroom teaching jobs in secondary schools, but many of us would send out dozens and dozens of applications and receive nothing in return.

My friend Denise Oakie was one of the fortunate ones. She sent out dozens of applications, received nothing from most of them, but then was offered an interview teaching Grade 7, and this was before our training was even finished! Denise was a fine young teacher, and apparently interviewed very well, because she got the job and left Kingston a week or so before our school year ended, promising to come back for graduation and after her actual "kid teaching" ended at the end of June.

So, I wasn't surprised when I saw her in downtown Kingston early in July. Most of my teaching friends had left town after graduation, and, except for my professors and a couple new teacher candidates who came to town two months early for the next school year, I knew almost nobody in town. I was pleased to see Denise and ran across the street to give her a big hug.

"Denise! How are you? How was teaching your very own class of Grade 7s?"

After a quick hug, she grabbed me by the lapels, pulling my face to within a few inches of hers and, in a kind of desperation, almost shouted, "Dave! They're not real people!"

I have no idea what happened to Denise after that meeting, what kind of career she enjoyed, if she stayed in the elementary panel or moved over to secondary. That was the last time I saw her. But her desperate shout confirmed for me what I'd always believed but didn't really know. I was meant to teach teenagers and not elementary school children.

I was good with teenagers: teenagers in big groups, teenagers in small groups, teenagers by themselves. With *little* kids—kids, say, five or six years old—I would be pretty good too, in small groups or singly, and for short periods of time. I had no actual evidence to support this. I'd never actually been with any small kids, but I could *imagine* being with them in small groups. I could not imagine being with eleven- or twelve-year-olds.

There was something about my memories of that time of life that informed this idea in me. Hormones running wild. Big fish in small ponds. Thinking that you had everything figured out. First crushes. Fragile, fragile egos. And adults never seeming to get any of it.

Nope. I was going to stay away from all of that.

I taught for one day—one—in an elementary school, in my whole *teaching* career. I'd been an occasional teacher for a few years and had gained a reputation among the ladies who called us out for teaching assignments each morning as a person who would go anywhere they needed me to go. They repaid me for this willingness by giving me choices when choices were available and by giving me long-term assignments of more than a couple weeks when they were available too.

"Dave, we've run out of elementary supply teachers. I know this is unusual, but could you teach a Grade 7/8 split class for us today? It would really help us out."

I thought back immediately to Denise Oakie and "They're not real people!" and thought for a few seconds before saying, "Sure . . . I guess . . . No problem."

"We're calling you late, we know, so we'll call the school to let them know that you have to be late, but that you're doing us all a favour, okay? But get there as soon as you can."

My car broke down on the way to the school. This was before the era of cell phones, but also before the era of telephone booths disappearing. You might not believe it, but there were actual phone booths, the kinds you've seen in Superman comics that had actual payphones in them, which only cost a quarter, and, usually, phone books too—books that contained the phone numbers of schools you were late for.

I called the principal, apologizing profusely, "Stupid car!" and then she actually came to pick me up.

As we drove to the school, she said, "Thanks for filling in on such late notice, Mr. Garlick. I don't know what we'd have done if you weren't available. There's no one with the kids right now. The teacher across the hall has left her door open. She's been looking in on them, but it's definitely not been optimal."

Despite what the principal had said, when I finally arrived at the classroom, the door was closed and locked.

A quick look through the window showed me that the class was out of control. Kids were standing on desks, paper balls and paper airplanes were flying around the room, and one girl was running back and forth at the front of the classroom, chalk in hand, drawing a continuous chalk line, back and forth across the board.

"I'm sorry," said the teacher across the hall. "I turned my back for a few seconds and one of the little bas—well, one of the children closed and locked the door. My key doesn't work on that door, and I didn't want to leave my class alone."

"No worries," I said. "The principal's given me a key."

"Good luck. You're gonna need it."

I unlocked the door, stepped into the room, and closed the door behind me. I *watched* a young girl wind up and throw a paper ball in my general direction. I stuck two fingers in my mouth and whistled one of those sharp, loud whistles your father probably used to call you home for supper or when the streetlights came on.

The class froze.

I pointed at the young girl who'd thrown the paper ball in my direction.

"Miss, you can pick that up, right now."

"You're always picking on me!" she whined.

"How can I always be doing *anything*, when I just walked in the door?"

At this piece of logic, she threw herself on the ground and began to beat on the floor, like a Looney Tunes character from the cartoons of my youth.

"Stop that!" I said sharply.

"She always does that, sir," said a boy who was actually sitting at his desk.

"No she doesn't! At least not today! Stop that and get up!"

"I can't have a tantrum?" she asked.

"No. Get up and go get that piece of paper."

"I don't have to pick up all of them, do I?"

"Just the one you threw. The one I saw you throw."

"Oh, okay."

I watched her pick up the paper and place it in the wastebasket.

"Now, if everyone can pick up one piece of paper, the room should be clean, right?" I asked.

Almost everyone got up to follow my instruction. One boy continued to sit in his seat.

"That's not fair," he said. "Not all of us threw papers. Why should those of us that didn't throw paper have to pick paper up? You're not being fair."

"Hmmm . . . I guess you're right. Being honest," I asked, "which of you didn't throw any paper?"

No one's hand went up. Not even the boy who told me I was being unfair.

"You're being unfair again," the boy said. "You're asking us to tell on each other. You're asking us to be finks."

"Not at all. I'm only asking those that were *good*, and not throwing paper around when the teacher wasn't here, to step up and take some pride in being good."

The whole time that the boy and I were having our discussion of ethics, the class, as a whole, had stopped to listen. The only person who kept moving was the girl who'd thrown the paper ball and who was satisfied with only being asked to pick up the one paper ball. She was quietly continuing to pick up planes and balls of paper.

"But kids might not want to admit to being good! They might be accused by some of us of being Goody-Two-Shoes! You're setting those kids up to be bullied—"

"Jason, you can stop," said the girl. "I've picked them all up. And you can't call me a Goody-Two-Shoes, because everyone saw me throw the ball at teacher! You're welcome, sir."

That's how my day *started*. Like Denise said, they weren't real people.

To be fair though, there were lots of high school kids who could also be accused, over the years, of not being real people. Some of my friends aren't real people. There are days I'm pretty sure I'm not very real either.

As a principal, on a few occasions, I was asked to be principal for a day in one of our elementary schools. This was only a few years ago, and by then I'd found out that I was actually pretty good with *all* kinds of people—not just teenagers. I was good with most teachers, most parents, most grandparents, and most school neighbours. Why shouldn't I also be pretty good with *kids*? And so, I looked forward to being principal for a day when it happened.

I gave kids high fives and low fives as they entered the building. I had kindergarten kids follow me down the hallway, all of us pretending to be airplanes. I spoke to Grade 8 kids about what high school was really like.

"No, no one is going to stuff you into a locker." "I guess *some* students might call you 'minor niners.'" "No, no teacher is going to stop you from dating a boy or girl in Grade 10 or 11." "Yes, you only have four classes a day."

At the end of recess, one of the youngest students in the school asked me for a hug, and when I actually gave him one, he gave me the biggest smile in return and latched onto my leg.

"Hang on, kid!" I told him. "You're going for a ride!"

Then I took giant strides down the hall with him hanging on, laughing.

"STOP! This is my classroom! Let me introduce you to my teacher! This is Mrs. Ackoy!"

Mrs. *McCoy* smiled and shook my hand. "I'm Dorothy McCoy. Thanks for delivering Clarence to class for me!"

"My pleasure, ma'am!" I said, tipping a pretend hat at her. "Have a nice afternoon, Clarence!"

"Thanks for the ride and the hug, mister!"

And my whole day was like that! I *was* good with kids!

My only other experiences with groups of young kids were when I was invited to be a "celebrity reader" at our neighbourhood elementary schools, always for junior kindergarten classes, and "celebrity judge" at neighbourhood speech contests, with kids from Grades 4 and up. As a judge, I had to pretend to be serious, but I always commended every student and told them how brave they were to stand up in front of a large group of people and deliver a speech. I told them, honestly, that after *death*, speaking in front of a group of people was the greatest fear for most people.

"More than being bitten by a rabid wolf?" I was once asked.

"Well, most people don't consider that, to be honest," I responded, thinking, They're not real people!

But being a celebrity reader was one of my greatest joys as a principal. I'd always bring along *Caps for Sale*, the story of a travelling cap seller, who goes to sleep under a tree in what I've always assumed was the countryside in Southern France or Italy, only to wake up to find that a troop of monkeys had stolen all his caps and were wearing them in the tree. The author avoided any explanation as to why there was a troop of monkeys in Southern France or Italy.

Anyway, I brought along the book, which had never been read by any of the four-year-olds I was reading to, along with my extensive collection of caps. I walked into the class balancing all the caps on my head, just as the Italian or French hero of the story did, and the kids would lose their minds! I'd carefully walk through the classroom, trying hard to not have the caps fall all over the place, but it didn't make any real difference if they did.

This was entertainment! the kids all thought. This was better than anything they'd ever seen in their whole *lives*! I imagined them all thinking.

The teacher or the principal would introduce me, the kids would gather around me on the floor, and I'd read the story. I encouraged them all to pretend to be monkeys and *steal* one of my caps, putting it on their head, and dance around the room like monkeys. They stamped on the ground when I stamped on the ground, shook their fists at me when I shook my fists at them, in their first ever monkey see, monkey do experience, and then in the twist that none of them ever saw coming, I had them all throw their caps to the ground when I threw my one remaining cap to the ground.

It brought down the house! The kids laughed and laughed. Who knew fine literature could be so much fun? And just when the kids were at their most wound up, laughing and continuing to pretend to be monkeys, discussing plot development, the man versus nature conflict of the story, perhaps the main character could have been developed a bit more, and what, exactly, *was* the theme? I'd have to leave. I'd apologize to the teacher, a bit disingenuously, because winding the kids up *was* my intent. Just like a weird but favourite uncle dropping the nephews and nieces off after an afternoon of fun and frivolity, for the parents to have to calm down.

And I know that the teachers watched me leave thinking, High school principals are not real people!

The Wisdom of My Superiors

There was a time, well, many more than *one* time, that I questioned the decisions and decision-making of my superintendents and directors. I don't remember ever questioning their wisdom. Though maybe I did. Certainly, when the director gifted us all with paperweights, five-pointed metal stars that weighed about a half pound, and told us he'd like to see them on our desks when he visited, I questioned his decision-making—and probably his wisdom. When you remember that, often, a principal's office is the site of conversations between two kids who had just been in a fight, giving them access to a five-pointed object with some heft, probably is not the wisest thing to do.

Anyway, every year, when you're a principal or vice-principal, senior administration—the superintendents and director—ask for your input as to what you'd prefer to happen with you and your team for the coming year. When I was a vice-principal, I never offered them my opinion. For the first two years, I didn't feel qualified to offer my opinion, nor did I think it very politic to offer it. Who was I to tell them anything? And at the end of my third year, I knew I was to be promoted, and it would have been the height of hubris to tell them where I thought they should send me.

As my first year as principal was ending though, I felt comfortable in saying, "Please leave us alone. I have a good team." I'd had two very experienced vice-principals, great at their jobs.

But, in their wisdom, senior admin transferred both of them, and I was assigned two new VPs: Angela Safranyos and Norm Ross. Again, though, we made a fine team, and Angela and Norm were two of my favourite VPs. Norm had been a brand-new VP and turned out to be one of the very best.

At the end of that year: "Please leave us alone. We make a good team." Nope. Angela was transferred, and I got another brand-new VP in Hazel Keefner. Again, though, we made a fine, fine team. I loved working with Norm and Hazel, and I think they truly loved working with me.

"Please leave us alone. We make a fine team, and I'd like one year of continuity."

I think you can see where this is going. I was never listened to. Each year though, things usually worked out at least all right. The year that I was transferred back to Forster from Western, I trusted that things would turn out at least all right then too.

That turned out to be an understatement. I was teamed up with John Foot. John was certainly the best VP I ever had, and I've never had to argue with anyone that he may have been the best VP in our system. I have no way of ranking him above or below the VPs that preceded us, but I'm pretty confident that he would be among the very best ever.

I've never made any claim to have ever been the *best* anything. Somewhere else in this book you can read what I thought of myself as a vice-principal, and I always thought of myself as a pretty good teacher, but John was simply the best. Allowing me to work with him was, from my perspective, one of the best decisions ever made on my behalf.

John and I made an excellent team. We never had to discuss who would play "good cop" to the other's "bad cop." It just happened, moving into the roles as soon as it became clear what was needed. And John never questioned one of my decisions the same way I never questioned one of his. We were, I think, perfect for each other. Although, now that I think of it, that had far more to do with John than it did with me.

Imagine this (and remember, before I returned to Forster, I'd never even met the man). In July of 2008, the year I was transferred back to Forster, I went to the school to set up my office—move over my books and records, hang some pictures, put up some posters with inspirational sayings, that kind of thing. And then a couple things just for me: a postcard of my favourite painting, *The Execution of Lady Jane Grey*, by Paul Delaroche, and a picture postcard of Albert Camus, who, while not my favourite writer, reminded me daily to try to live in the moment. Few people in Canada have ever seen or heard of *The Execution of Lady Jane Grey*. It's not a very famous painting, but if you google it, you might see why I love it so much. When I came upon it in the National Gallery in England, it so moved me that I lost time. A half hour flashed by as I stood there with tears in my eyes. I won't bore you here with a description of the painting, but I will encourage you to google it, because I'm as confident that you aren't aware of the painting as I was that I was the only administrator, maybe in North America, with that postcard on my office wall. It may seem an odd choice to have in a principal's office, given the subject matter, a beautiful young woman, blindfolded and about to have her head chopped off, but no one ever commented on it, in a negative or questioning way, in all the years it was posted.

Whenever things got too intense for me as a principal, I'd look at those two postcards and they'd sort of *reset* me.

When I'd finished up my office, I went down the hall to see if the VP was there. Late in July, there is no necessity for either the principal or VP to be there, but I always enjoyed the quiet of the empty building, and often went in through much of July and August, sometimes completely by myself, so I had no reason to expect that Mr. Foot would be there.

But he was.

He too enjoyed the peace of the empty school building. I forget, mostly, what we spoke about that day. We probably shook hands, and he probably invited me to have a seat. His office was set up so that John could see through to the hallway outside his office, but visitors would look only at him, the tiny window above the air-conditioner behind him offering no view at all from where a guest sat.

I had no idea if he was happy with the idea of having to break in a new principal, or what he'd been told about me, both by staff who probably remembered me as the caring but, well, not very good VP from six years before, and by the principal I was replacing, who I suspected was not happy with being transferred away from Forster and John Foot. John and I probably laughed, because we laughed, literally, almost every time we spoke. But I *know* we spoke about the postcard of Albert Camus he had tacked to the wall next to his desk. I'd purchased mine at the British Museum in 1985. John had purchased his somewhere in Paris. He kept his posted for much the same reason as I did. I thought it quite a positive coincidence.

We continued our get-to-know-each-other-a-bit talk, probably making plans for dinner or a drink. It turned out that John and I also shared a love for food and enjoyed entertaining small groups of people at our homes. I thought, I'm going to like working with this man.

When I turned around to leave, I *knew* I was going to work well with John. Mounted on the wall, so that he could see it while he was talking with students or parents, teachers, or new principals was a poster of a painting. It was *The Execution of Lady Jane Grey.*

What were the chances of that?

Mitzy the Wonderdog

In case you're wondering, the picture above is not a picture of Mitzy the Wonderdog. It is a picture of a skunk. The reason for this will soon become apparent.

Mitzy was a great dog and a wonderful ambassador for dogdom. She was a twenty-pound, mostly black terrier, with one ear up and one ear down. She bore a striking resemblance to Toto from *The Wizard of Oz* but with longer legs. She was a celebrity in our neighbourhood. Kids would ask if they could pet her, dropping to their knees and rubbing their faces in her fur. It was clear she loved the attention. When she got her bimonthly grooming, she felt like velvet, and she loved to show off the new kerchief she received with each haircut. I remember her tugging me to Rob and Lynn's house two streets over to show them her kerchief, sitting politely when I rang their doorbell, and her tail wagging furiously when Lynn answered the door.

"Well! Who do we have here? Aren't you a beautiful little thing!"

She wasn't just a pretty face. A rescue dog from the Chatham pound, from the first day we brought her home and at maybe three years old the veterinarian thought, she asked politely to go out the back door and then barked once, just once, to be let back in.

She was, in almost all respects, a wonderful dog.

Her only issue was that, if she got out on her own, her nose went to the ground and all her other senses were turned off. There was a whole world out there to sniff. Nothing could turn her around. We were very fortunate not to lose her.

Our backyard was her dominion, and death waited for any animal that dared to venture into it. As a terrier, she was just doing her job, so we never got angry at her for this. She killed four rabbits, a rat, a possum, and several birds. She was never able to catch a squirrel, but she never tired of trying. The only animal she ever lost to—just the once, because, as I said, she wasn't just a pretty face—was a skunk.

This was at 5:00 one dark morning as I was getting ready to leave for a principals' conference. My morning routine never varied much: get out of bed without the need for an alarm, leave the lights off so as not to wake my wife, follow Mitzy down the stairs, let her out the back door, turn the coffee pot on, and put a couple of pieces of bread in the toaster. When the toast was ready, I'd spread it with peanut butter or cream cheese, and then let Mitzy in. Usually, we were able to time this so that she didn't have to bark even the once, but this morning, when I opened the door, she wasn't there.

Before I could even whisper-call for her, she shot up the steps, ran past me into the carpeted back room, and began rubbing her face against the carpet, clearly in distress. I ran to her and dropped to my knees. She jumped into my arms and threw up on me. It was only then that I smelled—something. I'd never smelled fresh skunk to that point, and you might be surprised to find out, as I was, that *fresh* skunk doesn't really smell like skunk. Acrid burnt metal or burned rubber, maybe. Really unpleasant, but not like skunk.

I forget how Linda was awakened to this. In any case, she and I were very soon bathing Mitzy in the kitchen sink, as it was clear that whatever had sprayed Mitzy got her full in the face. Our niece Lindsay was staying with us that week because we were taking her to Stratford to see a play or two as a graduation present. She, too, was pressed into service. In a few minutes, the actual crisis was over.

Mitzy calmed down, and as the smell outside aged, it became clear that the animal that had changed my morning routine was indeed a skunk.

Now, if you've been paying attention as you've been reading, you'll know that our back room now smelled of skunk, as did our kitchen, Mitzy of course, me, Linda, and Lindsay. I went upstairs to shower, dress, and finish packing my clothes for the weekend. My friend and fellow principal, Al Timmins, was going to pick me up shortly after 6:00, along with Josh Canty and Manny Novelletto—in a brand-new, rented car.

When they arrived, I volunteered to drive myself, but as good friends sometimes do, they said, "It's not that bad." (It was.) "The smell will dissipate." (It didn't.) "If things *do* get bad, we can always drive with the windows down." (It was too cold.) Thankfully, though, our olfactory senses all shut down, as they will, out of mercy. After a few very unpleasant minutes and some very bad jokes, we no longer smelled anything.

We stopped at a small-town diner, in Watford, for breakfast. As we entered, it was clear that my shower and the two-hour drive had not changed much to the way that I smelled. Patrons all turned to look at us as we entered. I put my hand up immediately. "I'm sorry. It's me. My dog got sprayed by a skunk this morning and jumped into my arms."

"A skunk jumped into your arms?" This was an old man in a red flannel jacket and a Massey-Ferguson baseball cap.

"No, sir. My dog jumped into my arms."

"Oh. Dog okay?"

"Yes, sir. She's fine."

"That's okay then."

People went back to eating their breakfasts.

I repeated the "It's me. I'm sorry" line again when we got to the hotel to register and later when we went to the principals' mixer. Two of my superintendents thought it was hilarious and made several of the same bad jokes that Al, Josh, and Manny had made a few hours earlier.

I showered after the mixer, again after dinner, and once more before going to bed. Hotel staff brought me a fan, I think at the suggestion of one of the other principals, and hotel staff arranged for me not to have to share a room with anyone. Or rather, hotel staff arranged for no one having to share a room with me.

By the next morning, I didn't really smell that bad anymore. There was a *hint*, a *reminder,* of the experience about me, but you had to get pretty close and actually smell me, sniffing in the same way Mitzy would have, to notice, which is what I asked of my friends Hazel Keefner, Mary Edwards, and Angela Safranyos.

"Hey. Ladies? Smell me, please. Do I still smell of skunk?"

"A bit, Dave. A bit. It's not that bad, really," they each answered.

Because I was feeling pretty sorry for myself the last two days, I didn't even think of what my wife and niece were going through. A few hours after I left home, they had an appointment in a bank to set up a bank account for Lindsay. They too had to go through the "It's me. I'm sorry" experience as people moved away from them as they waited. They then had to watch the banker pretend not to care or notice. "No. Really. If you hadn't said anything, I wouldn't even have noticed. Would you mind if I opened the door?"

Like me, they each showered multiple times through the day, scrubbed the backroom carpet, and took Mitzy into the basement to bathe her multiple times with Dawn dishwashing soap, which the internet will tell you is far more effective than the famous-for-no-real-reason tomato juice, though they used that too.

By the end of the day, they too smelled far better, with only the *hint* or *reminder* about themselves. Mitzy smelled better, but because she was sprayed in the face, and Linda and Lindsay didn't want to get soap in her eyes and nose and mouth, the smell hung there for literally weeks, months, when she got wet in the rain.

On Saturday, Linda and I had arranged for us to meet in a small town, I forget which one. Al, Josh, and Manny would drop me off before continuing home, and Linda and Lindsay would pick me up before heading to Stratford. It worked perfectly. I only had time to drink a coffee at Tim Horton's before Linda and Lindsay arrived.

We shared our embarrassing stories, Linda expressing huge relief that the kennel didn't mind taking a dog with a *hint* or *reminder* of an incident with a skunk. Again, though, it was Mitzy, and the staff all loved her there. By this point, we could mostly laugh at the experience.

However, when we got to the hotel that afternoon and opened our luggage, we were all reminded that we'd packed *after* Mitzy had been sprayed, but *before* we'd each showered four or five times. Our dress clothes, as nice as they looked, *smelled* of Mitzy's encounter. Hotel staff were sympathetic and uncomplaining. And *maybe* we were sensitive to it, and it didn't smell as bad as we thought.

We had front row seats at the theatre that evening for *King Lear*. We were worried that maybe they'd stop the play and demand we leave, but the actors there are consummate professionals, who live by the dictum, "the Show Must Go On," so no one even appeared to notice, though we all apologized to everyone around us.

"It's us, we're sorry."

We drove back to Windsor after the play, talking more about Stratford and the plays we'd seen than Mitzy and her episode with the skunk. The kennel was still open when we got back to Windsor, so we were able to pick her up on the way home. She sat on my lap, and, though she rarely "kissed" anyone, she did lick my face once when she jumped into the car.

"Hon? I think the kennel gave her a bath or two. She doesn't smell at all!"

"Really? Let's see. Mitzy, do you want to go home?"

Mitzy jumped into her lap and kissed her once too.

"David Garlick, you *lied* to me! She still smells of skunk!"

"I didn't think it fair that I'd be the only one to experience that for the rest of the ride home."

Lindsay and I both laughed. Linda didn't think it was funny.

It was at least a couple weeks until I let the neighbourhood kids pet Mitzy on our morning walks.

Desks

My desks have always been a mess, whether at home or at work. As a fifteen-year-old boy, I purchased a roll-top desk and carefully stained and Varathaned it myself. Even then, I appreciated the fact that I'd be able to roll the top closed and hide the mess underneath. As a vice-principal and principal, I never had that option, and so, my desk was, as I said, a mess.

Occasionally, I'd try cleaning it up. After students had gone home, I'd spend a couple hours assembling neat-looking piles and throwing out a few things from the ministry or unsolicited mail. Sometimes, I'd quickly slide things into a drawer I'd designated for such a purpose, but usually, it was just a mess.

At home, if my wife pestered me about the look of my desk, I simply closed the roll top to appease her. She knew better than to ask me to actually clean out the drawers, because whenever that happened it became a full-day event. I'd have to relate why I'd kept a linen napkin for thirty years. Show her, again, the signed photographs of Al Kaline and Mickey Lolich, along with any number of things that would never be thrown away, like my grandfather's harmonica from World War I.

Although my desk gave every appearance of being a mess, and I confess that it was, I actually knew where almost everything was. If you asked for a particular piece of correspondence, I could find it for you in seconds, usually quicker than someone who had filed it away using their own system. My first principal, Elver Peruzzo, didn't believe this and would sometimes test me, just for fun. But even though he never caught me out, he still didn't approve of the look of my desk.

"Dave, it just creates the wrong impression. You have to think of appearances."

One day, when I was away at a vice-principals' meeting, he organized my desk for me. To do this, he simply created twelve piles of paper, straightened them up, and placed them in file folders. When I returned the next morning, he was waiting at my office door, still quite pleased with himself and certain I would be as pleased as he was.

"It looks very organized, doesn't it? Think of the impression it creates!"

"And what impression will it create when I can't find anything?"

"If you ever want to be a principal, you're going to have to keep a clean-looking desk."

"Elver, I'm not even sure I want to be a *vice*-principal."

Anyway, it turned out that he was wrong. I was a principal for fourteen years and almost never had a clean-looking desk.

My second principal certainly had a clean desk. He had a rule that there was never to be more than three pieces of paper on his desk at day's end.

"How do you do it?" I asked, genuinely interested and hoping for a system I could use.

"Simple. See this drawer? At the end of each day, I just scoop everything off the top of my desk and throw it in here."

My first VP showed his desk off to me, although I hadn't asked him. "I try to keep it organized and neat. Once each week, I close the door, turn on a timer, and devote an hour to making it look like this." This was in August, before the school year began, and my desk hadn't had the chance to acquire its usual messiness, so I think he thought he was talking to a kindred spirit.

"What's the old cookie jar for?" I asked. It was an old, tin cookie jar, clearly not being used for cookies.

"That's my collection of confiscated marijuana."

"Pardon?"

He opened it to show me.

"Richard! There must be sixty or seventy joints in there!"

"Yeah, well, I've been collecting them since I became a VP."

"You know this means you're in possession of a significant amount of pot, right? I mean, *probably* no police officer would charge you, but—"

"But it wasn't mine!"

"It *has* been yours, some of it for more than a few years, right?'

"I never thought of it like that."

So, we spent the next ten minutes flushing it down the toilet.

The next VP in that office had a very similar desk philosophy to mine. So he was quite proud on his first day to show off his neat desk top.

"What do you think?" he asked.

There was absolutely nothing on it, except in the middle of the desk, closest to where I was sitting and where every student would be sitting, was a large, white marble clock. It probably weighed up to ten pounds and sported some very sharp edges.

"You're going to have to move that," I said, pointing to the clock.

"Why? It was a going away present from the kids at Walkerville."

"This is why." I picked it up and pretended I was going to smash his head with it.

"Oh."

Years later, when we were both closer to retirement, a new director started his tenure with our board by giving us each a paperweight at the last principals' meeting of the year. They were metal stars, emblazoned with a positive message I've forgotten. They weighed almost a pound and sported five very sharp points.

"It would be nice if I saw these on your desks when I visit your schools next year," he said.

My former VP, now an experienced principal himself, smiled at me and said, "Not likely. Maybe it'll see my desk at home."

By the way, although I've been quite open about the messy state of my desks over the years, not one student, parent, or teacher ever commented on it in a negative way. Just my first principal.

However, a few months after I'd left Western and returned to Forster, I was talking with one of my former teachers in a grocery store.

"Dave, you should see the new principal's desk! There's never *anything* on it! I mean nothing! Not even a telephone! He polishes it every day! It's creepy! No one wants to go in there! And not just kids. None of us! It's not natural!

I guess it was meant as a compliment to me.

Of sorts.

I guess.

The Comfort of Finding Out, for Certain, That the Kids Do Come First

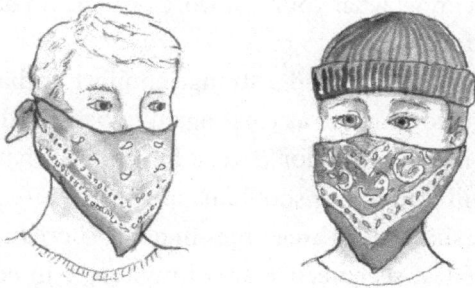

The weather was terrible that night. Sleet had been falling for a couple hours, and the road was ice-glazed. Even though I wasn't driving very fast, my car hit a patch of ice and began to fishtail. I saw the truck barreling down the highway towards me and realized we were very likely going to collide, and I was very likely going to die. There was little I could do to avoid it.

"Shit, shit, shit!" I said. Three times. In quick succession.

Although counterintuitive, I thought that, maybe, the only thing I could do to avoid an accident that would surely kill me was turn *towards* the truck and try to make it to the shoulder on the other side of the two-lane highway.

Which is what I did, slamming on the brakes when I felt and heard the gravel shoulder under my wheels. The truck continued on, its horn no longer blowing, and its driver, I'm sure, glad he hadn't killed the person in the beat-up, old car.

I sat there, my heart rate slowly returning to normal, my grip on the steering wheel slowly loosening. I came close to crying in relief but then started laughing.

"Look at it this way, Dave," I said to myself. "At least now you know what your last words will be if you die in a car accident."

I found and still find a strange comfort in that knowledge. I've never come as close again to being killed in my car but have known for a very long time what my last words will be if it ever should happen.

"Shit, shit, shit." Three times in quick succession.

In the last seventeen years of my career in education, at least once or twice a year, I was involved in a group discussion about lockdowns and shooters in the school. This always happened during staff meetings dealing with the procedures to follow for tornadoes, fire alarms, and lockdowns.

"Dave, you say that in the event of a lockdown being called, we're supposed to look into the hall, and if we see any students out there, we're to drag them into our classrooms. But what if one of those kids *is* the shooter?"

"Well, if that's the case, you're probably going to die. But, obviously, I hope that never happens."

Once, just once, a teacher said, "That's easy for you to say. You'll be safe in your office, waiting for the police."

I just looked at him, not believing someone would accuse me of that.

"I'm sorry Dave. I didn't mean that. Talking about this stuff just makes me crazy."

Another teacher then added, "If there's ever a shooter in the building, Dave's probably going to be the one that gets shot!"

"Thanks. I think. I guess that's a compliment, right?" And then everyone laughed, the tension broken, until the conversation happened again the next year.

Although it was *nice* that some staff thought I'd place myself in harm's way if there were an active shooter in the school, and I actually *thought* that I would, I also hoped that I would never find out.

I thought about it often though. It was likely that if there were a shooter, it would be a student from the school; someone I would know and someone, I hoped, who would like me and not want to shoot me. I'd approach them, I thought, hands out but not up, using their name, being as calm as I could. Asking them to put the gun down or use me as a hostage.

I ran through the scenarios again and again in my mind.

But I never actually *knew* how I'd behave. Maybe I *would* cower in my office with the door locked.

Then my last semester in school began. I announced to the staff that I was retiring at the end of the year and asked them to not let the kids know just yet. And then, as my wife has often said, all Hell broke loose for no real reason.

Two anonymous shooting threats in a bit more than a month that involved the police and superintendents and newspaper articles and phone calls from concerned parents. Then, an actual shooting not far from the building and the police putting us into a "hold and secure," locking the doors and letting no one in or out. Plus, the suicide of a former student in his thirties late on a Sunday evening, in our parking lot behind the school.

We were all on edge. Geez, I thought. Just let me get to the end of the school year!

Being with the kids, though, usually took the edge off. At lunch, I'd trade jokes with the kids outside, picking up garbage and telling the smokers, all seven or eight of them, that they should quit. Having a good time each day.

Then, "Hey, sir? What are those two guys doing over there?"

I looked in the direction the young man was pointing and saw two other young men wearing masks walking slowly towards the school. This was long before COVID. Masks were very out of the ordinary. And this was late May. There was no good reason I could think of for two men to be walking towards us wearing masks.

"Hey kids?" I said to the smokers. "Do me a favour, okay? Please don't argue with me, and please walk back towards the school, okay? Don't run, please just walk, okay? And tell the first teacher you see to call the police."

There was no argument, and I was very happy. I took out my phone, turned on the camera, and started walking towards the two men. And just loudly enough, I said, "Can I help you, gentlemen? What can I do for you?"

But I was thinking, So if I ever get shot at school, I know what my last words will be and that I really will put myself in harm's way for the kids. I hope I get to retire though.

And then the two *hombres* pulled off their masks and started laughing in a very embarrassed way. Two of my all-time favourite kids. I never did find out why they were wearing masks in the first place, but knowing them, it had to do with having just watched *Butch Cassidy and the Sundance Kid,* or they were rehearsing a scene for a play, doing research to see how it felt. They apologized in case they'd caused me any concern.

I didn't cry in relief, although I felt like it. I did laugh though. Quietly. And just as quietly, said to myself, "Shit, shit, shit."

Three times. In quick succession.

Part Four:
David in Retirement

3:00 a.m. Hypochondria

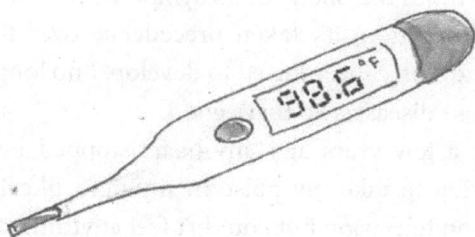

I am a 3:00 a.m. hypochondriac. Admittedly, as neuroses go, this is one of the least debilitating. It's not keeping me from enjoying my life. It's not keeping me from "the promotion," and it's not keeping me from forming and maintaining lasting and fulfilling personal relationships. It is, however, by definition, keeping me up at night.

Lately, it's been COVID. At 3:00, I wake up certain that I've contracted it somehow. The first time, it was a dry throat. "Well, this isn't normal," I said to myself. I didn't wake up my wife and haven't awakened her on subsequent nights either. I mean, what's she going to do about it? Talking with her only increases the chances of giving it to her. I wonder if I should move to the guest bedroom. No, that will only wake her up and then she'll worry about me having COVID. Will I have to go to the hospital in the morning? Is my will up to date? No, it's not, I'll have to take care of that from the hospital. Do I have a clean pair of underwear? If I drive myself to the hospital, where should I park the car?

I fall asleep with these questions running through my mind, and in the morning, I no longer have COVID.

I've had COVID six or seven times at 3:00 a.m. so far. A couple times the one with no symptoms.

As a condition, it's taken precedence over the brain cancer and skin cancer I used to develop. I no longer seem to get those diseases. So that's good.

Once, a few years ago, my heart stopped beating at 3:00. I tried to take my pulse in my neck like I've seen them do on television but couldn't feel anything. I put my hand right on my chest over my heart and couldn't feel anything there either. I even put my head to my pillow, which sometimes keeps me from falling asleep at ten or eleven o'clock, because I hate listening to my heartbeat in the pillow. It makes me wonder if that's normal and if maybe I've suddenly developed high blood pressure, and maybe I'm going to have a stroke during the night and die. Anyway, even the pillow thing didn't reveal a still-beating heart.

All I felt was a vague sort of buzzing, like I had a small hive of bees in my chest.

"Hey, hon? Hon? Are you awake?"

"I am now. What is it?"

"I think my heart's stopped beating."

She chuckled. God bless the man who can make his wife laugh after waking her up at three in the morning to tell her his heart has stopped beating.

"Well, if it *has* stopped beating, I don't think you'd be talking to me right now," she said.

Point taken, I guess. "But I don't have a pulse, and I just have this vague sort of buzzing, like there's a hive of bees in my chest."

She put her ear to my chest, which felt pretty nice at three-something in the morning, even if my heart had stopped. "You have a strong, regular heartbeat."

"Well, that's good."

"Maybe you should call the doctor in the morning. You've been pretty stressed at work lately."

I didn't ask her if she meant I should ask the doctor about my worry about my heart or whether I should ask him about my *worry* about my heart, but I guess it didn't really matter.

The doctor gave me a Holter device to wear, which monitored my heartbeat for two days and gave me the opportunity to explain what it was to my students, my colleagues, and my principal and to tell them all that the doctor thought that maybe I was stressed. Everyone was a bit nicer to me for the next couple days, and a week later, the doctor told me that all my readings were normal.

My heart never stopped beating again, which allowed my hypochondria to give me brain cancer and skin cancer instead, which I guess was a bit of an improvement.

Now that I'm getting COVID some nights, I wonder if that means I'm cured of the brain cancer and skin cancer?

That would be a good thing.

Kid, Your Dad Knows Everybody

Before I tell you this story, you have to know two things: first, when I was a kid, my father knew everybody. Not just the people on the street, which you'd expect, but *every*body. When we bought gas, he knew the man who pumped it. When we went to the grocery store, he knew the butcher and the checkout lady. They knew him too. By name.

"Hi, Stan! How you doin' today?"

"Oh, pretty good, Lester."

That kind of thing. The people who worked in the bank, the people who worked at the movie theatre—everybody.

Once, when we were on vacation in Prince Edward Island, literally more than a thousand miles from home, at a campground, Dad was looking off in the distance and said, more to himself than anybody, but I was standing next to him, "Hey! I think that's Stinky Ledbetter!"

And then, in a voice loud enough for everyone in the campground to hear, maybe everybody in Prince Edward Island, Dad yelled, "Hey! Stinky! Stinky Ledbetter!"

I was mortified. How could it possibly be Stinky Ledbetter? How would a man get such a nickname, and surely, even if it *was* Stinky Ledbetter, he wouldn't answer to my father's shouting, this far from home. Surely, this far from home he deserved to escape his nickname.

"Stink!"

I was twelve years old, and I had never been more embarrassed in my life. "Dad! Geez! Stop!"

"What? That's Stinky Ledbetter!"

And then Stinky Ledbetter was talking to my dad and tousling my hair. "I was kind of shocked to see your father this far from home, but I guess I shouldn't've been. Your dad knows everybody, kid."

The other thing you need to know, before I tell this story, is that my dad is *really* hard of hearing. He has been for most of my life. Surgeries didn't help much, and he's worn two hearing aids for decades.

For the time being, I ask you to think that these two attributes, my father knowing everybody and also being hard of hearing, are completely unrelated.

Anyway, as I grew up, went to school, got a job at McDonald's, and then went to university, I too began to know a few people. More still when I went away to teachers' college and then started teaching. After a few years, I always ran into people who I knew, or who knew me, at the mall or at the grocery store.

"Hi Mr. Garlick! You probably don't remember me, but you taught me a hundred years ago."

"Hi, Dave! I haven't seen you since our McDonald's days! Fun times, eh?"

I grew to expect it and am always a little disappointed if a trip to the mall doesn't result in at least one such meeting.

And I, too, have run into friends accidentally, both in Prince Edward Island and also in England! Not Stinky Ledbetter, mind you, but Craig Bennett and his wife Yvonne in PEI, and Bob Gillies in England. Really!

At some point, I came to realize that, at least in that one respect, I had become my father.

So, it came as no surprise to me yesterday, when I went to visit my father in the hospital (he's going to be fine, don't worry), that I was stopped by a woman who said, "Dave? Dave Garlick?"

We were both wearing masks, which was the only reason she wasn't sure it was me, and the only reason I didn't recognize Lorie Schofield immediately. Lorie was my first attendance secretary when I was a brand-new vice-principal, twenty-three years ago. Lorie was with her father, and they were at the hospital to visit Lorie's mother, who is also going to be okay. She'd fallen and struck her head against a coffee table, giving herself a nice shiner. Hospital staff were concerned about a possible concussion.

We talked for a bit, and Lorie introduced me to her father.

"Garlick?" he asked. "Would you be related to a Stan Garlick?"

"Yes I would! Stan's my father! I'm here to visit him."

"Gee! I used to work with Stan at Chrysler's. That was a long time ago! Please tell him Norm Laframboise says hi and that I hope he gets better soon. I haven't thought of your father in, what, maybe sixty years!"

As I took the elevator to my father's room, I thought that this had never happened before. I ran into someone *I* knew, and the person she was with knew my father! I know everybody, so many that some of them also know my dad!

Windsor is *this* big! I thought, holding an imaginary thumb an inch from an imaginary forefinger. This'll be a great story to tell my father. It's sure to cheer him up!

So when I got to his room and we'd exchanged the normal pleasantries you exchange in the hospital— "How are you feeling? Is the food okay? Have they told you anything about when they might release you?—I asked him, "Dad, do you remember a man named Norm Laframboise?"

"Who?"

"Norm Laframboise. He told me he worked with you at Chrysler's. So that would have been more than sixty years ago."

"Is he still alive?"

"Yes! I was just talking with him! His daughter used to work with me at Lowe!"

"Isn't that something? Gee, he must be near to ninety now!"

"Yup. Just like you!

"Y'know, I've sometimes wondered if he was still alive. Isn't that something? Al Watts . . ."

"Who? No. Norm Laframboise. Not Al Watts."

"Al Watts is what I called him."

Almost all my dad's friends and co-workers had nicknames: Johnny Nine Fingers. Stinky Ledbetter. Dirty Alfie. I never asked him how the nicknames were acquired. Every once in a while, he'd offer up an explanation without being asked.

"You know how Johnny Nine Fingers got his name, right?"

"I'm guessing he lost a finger?"

Dad would be disappointed that I'd guessed it right off, but then he'd get to tell us the tale of how, in this case, Johnny lost the finger. For my dad, that was just about as good. The explanations were usually pretty harrowing or disgusting.

So I wasn't surprised that Norm Laframboise would have a nickname, but "Al Watts" didn't seem particularly harrowing or disgusting. We talked for a bit more about Norm/Al.

"The last time I spoke to old Al Watts was about thirty years ago," my father reflected. "His wife had had a terrible stroke and was confined to her bed."

This didn't fit with the little I'd just learned about Lorie's mother, who had fallen and hit her head.

"Well, either he married again, or his wife got better. She's downstairs in Emergency right now."

"Who is?"

"Norm's wife. Lorie's mother. She fell down."

"Lorie fell down?"

"NO! LORIE'S MOTHER! NORM'S WIFE!" Conversations with my father usually become sessions where I yell, and then Dad pretends to hear.

"Oh. But he's going to be okay, right?"

"SHE! NORM'S WIFE!"

"Oh."

I had a thought. "How did Norm get the nickname Al Watts?"

Dad stared at me. This always means that he didn't hear.

"HOW DID NORM GET THE NICKNAME AL WATTS?"

"It was his name."

I took a piece of paper and wrote out the name Norm Laframboise, holding it up for him to read.

"Who's that?"

"THAT'S THE MAN I MET DOWNSTAIRS."

He studied the piece of paper and read the name out loud a couple times. "I don't think I know him, but gee . . . Imagine you meeting Al Watts!"

A Man of the Past

This piece, on aging or getting older, is longer than I expected it to be when I started. It kind of meanders too, like a small stream, slowly drying in the fall. I find it fitting, and although that wasn't my intention when I started, I like it. My friends who are older than I am, and I have many, might be a bit bothered by the fact that I, so much their junior, am thinking I am getting older, but here's the thing: it doesn't bother me in the least. I don't think of any of my friends as old. I like the age I am. I like every age I've been. The fact that some things have changed in ways that bother me is a part of getting older. The fact that I think of the music of my youth as superior to the music of today is no different than kids today thinking their music is superior.

It's just the way things are.

I remember, for a short time being our school board's "Golden Boy." At thirty-four, I was the youngest department head in the system. I was then the youngest vice-principal in a secondary school and then the youngest principal. And then, almost overnight it seemed, I was the board's senior secondary school principal and accepting a clock from our director as I retired.

My friend and former student Rana used to gently make fun of me by informing me that I was "no longer the youth of today." She started this when I was in my late thirties, and *she* was among the youth of the day. I'm *still* no longer the youth of today. I've become so old I don't even *know* if I appreciate kids' music, because I don't listen to it, and any attempt to pretend that I did would be exposed as a lie in seconds. I can honestly go only so far as to say that I find Taylor Swift and Dua Lipa attractive but can't name any of their songs.

Oh well. The fact is that Rana, too, is no longer the youth of today. I smile at this because, although she's married, a professional, and owns her second house, I still call her a kid.

Every student I worked with is now an adult. My dentist, Dr. Rista Urukalo, is a former student. She's almost old enough to be starting to think about retiring. Ali Awad is married with three children, one in high school, and he runs one of the most successful karate dojos in the area. Sarorn Sim is married, a father, and is an internationally respected cinematographer who owns a cutting-edge company repurposing old camera lenses for new cameras. I could go on and on. Several of my "kids" are now teachers and school administrators, for example.

So, I can take some pride in no longer being the youth of today but having influenced the next generations a bit. I am, now, a man of the past. Time and events seem to be conspiring to erase me. Writing is one way I've found to slow this process.

If we were to meet for the first time, or if you were a student of mine, who didn't really know me very well, and we were to meet at the Dominion House on Sandwich Street, I'd probably tell you that I grew up not far from here, that this was my old neighbourhood. I'd be telling you the truth, because as a kid, I walked to the "DH" and to my high school, which was just up the street a few blocks.

But as a West End kid, I'd be lying to you. Or at least, most other West Enders would tell you I was lying, because I grew up way over on Partington and Randolph Avenues, on the other side of the Ambassador Bridge, which is kind of like saying I lived on the other side of the tracks, almost two full kilometres away.

Although those West Enders would grudgingly admit that I was also a West Ender, they'd add the qualifier that I hadn't grown up in Sandwich. But neither had almost any of them, because the town of Sandwich legally ceased to exist in 1935 when it became part of Windsor, and all of us became simply West Enders. The old, white, bearded man at the end of the bar might be able to claim he was born in Sandwich, but he almost certainly would have few, in any, memories of the town.

He might remember me, though, because I was a regular at the DH from the time I was sixteen and an underage drinker. During most weeks from the time I turned sixteen, I spent at least a couple hours in the DH. Beer was only thirty cents a glass, later fifty cents, but still affordable for a kid like me.

Now, you might be saying to yourself, Sixteen! That's not right! But times were different back then. The *legal* age to drink was eighteen, but few bars checked your identification, and no one seemed to care very much. I only worried about being caught out the first couple times I went in, and I rarely drank enough to get drunk and draw attention to myself. The friends I went with to the DH were all underage as well. I remember the surprise on the manager's face when I went there to celebrate my eighteenth birthday. She gave me a free fifty-cent beer, knew me by name, and asked me how old I was. She looked shocked when I told her, but I've always had a bit of a baby face, so she must have had some suspicions.

Yup. Times were different, and times have changed. Things that once were no longer are.

My whole life in Windsor has been kind of like that. Many of the places where I grew up, or that were important to me, have ceased to exist. It's one of the reasons I asked to meet with you at the Dominion House and that I've volunteered for so long at the Duff-Baby House. They're among the few places that have refused to disappear or change very much, and I do my best to help them.

The neighbourhoods where I grew up have changed so much I barely recognize them. Both the apartment building we lived in, on Partington, and the first house my parents owned, on Randolph, have gone from being in comfortable middle-class neighbourhoods to being on streets that house university students mainly. Houses that once helped raise families of two, three, or four children, now hold seven, eight, or nine university students. Bedrooms that were shared by three boys or three girls have been carved up to hold as many adults, but individually, in much smaller spaces. Piles of empty pizza boxes on front porches have taken the place of children's bicycles, and many of the large maple trees that formed a canopy over the road in my youth have died.

The fields in which I once played all summer long, catching grasshoppers and garter snakes, have been replaced by affordable housing units. Many of these, too, are filled with university students.

My grade school, Prince of Wales, no longer exists. It closed down in the last century, was torn down in this one, and replaced by the University of Windsor's engineering building. My high school, John L. Forster Secondary, no longer exists either. I, the school's last principal, closed it in 2014. It now sits empty, mouldering in what once was a vibrant neighbourhood. Many of the houses I walked by each day, hoping one day to be well off enough to afford, have been either torn down or, like my old school, sit boarded up and deteriorating in a once vibrant neighbourhood. You might say that this is a coincidence of living in the West End so near the Ambassador Bridge, which, at close to a hundred years old, is under almost constant reconstruction. But the first school I was comfortably ensconced in, and wouldn't have been bumped from by a teacher senior to me at the end of the school year, Directions, on the city's *east* side, was also closed and then torn down, replaced by a number of small affordable houses.

From Directions, I was promoted to W.D. Lowe Secondary, one of Windsor's oldest and largest schools. I was a department head and became a vice-principal there. I helped close it in 2000.

The first school at which I was a principal, Western Secondary School, not even in Windsor but actually Amherstburg, closed two years ago. I'm beginning to think it has something to do with me, and not just time, age, or coincidence.

And it's not only buildings; it's traditions too. When I first became a vice-principal, almost the first week I *was* a vice-principal, I was invited to the retiring administrators' dinner. I forget who retired that year, but I was very pleased to see that each of them was honoured with an antique-looking teacher's hand bell, with their names and schools inscribed on it. I thought, What a perfect gift for a retiring principal! So much better than a gold watch. What retiree even *wants* a watch?

Although it wasn't a reason for me to stay on as a vice-principal and then a principal for seventeen years, I have to admit that it was something that I looked forward to receiving one day. When I went to Western Secondary School in 2002, I found out that the man who made the bells lived right across the street from the school. His forge was right across the street from the school.

I introduced myself to him and told him how much I liked his work and that I was looking forward to receiving one of his bells one day. He was pleased with that, and with me as his new neighbour, and we often waved to each other from across the street when I arrived at work. Then he had a stroke, died, his forge was sold, and the bells stopped being made.

Principals now receive a gold watch when they retire. Because of my annual whining about this, I was the last principal to receive a brass hand bell, not one made in Amherstburg to look like an antique, but a true antique, actually used at one time by a real teacher in a one room schoolhouse in the late nineteenth century. It was my last vice-principal, Theresa Williams, now a principal herself, who arranged for this.

The only school I've been associated with as a principal or vice-principal that's still open is Walkerville Secondary School, now Windsor's oldest school at a 101 years old. Another tradition was that principals, as they retire or leave a school, had their pictures framed and placed somewhere in the building. At Forster, it was at the entrance. At Walkerville, it was the library. (Note the use of the past tense.)

Shortly after I retired, I attended a ceremony at the school at which Leah Flynn, one of my favourite students, hung my picture on the wall of the library. I thought it symbolic and told her so. In addition to being one of my favourite students, she is also the granddaughter of my very first vice-principal, Ron Kerr, who was the VP of my grade school, when I was a student there in the 1960s. Kind of a full circle thing.

But then the school board decided to update the school, starting with the library, which now, despite being part of a 101-year-old building, looks more like a Starbuck's than a school library. It's beautiful, I admit, but there's no place for the photos of 101 years of principals. So, my picture no longer hangs in the school. I'd ask for it, but I'm afraid I'll be told that it was tossed out or shipped to the board office to their archives to rest along with everything else that is old and out of date.

Note: After I'd written the above paragraphs, just this morning in fact, I went back to Walkerville and found that the pictures of the old principals, me included, have been remounted in the library, but I'm leaving the above section in anyway. Just to make me feel old, I saw that only 3 of the principals in 101 years were from before my lifetime, and I've known all but 4, including those 3!

Times change.

I've been able, though, to still find activities and things to do at which I'm among the youngest. I volunteer for Goodfellows, for example, and I'm on their board, and one of the things we discuss each month is that we have to find a way of attracting younger volunteers. No one on the board looks at me when they say this. Pickleball is fun. Because of my writing, I've begun to teach at Unicom and Elder College, lifelong-learning programs offered to seniors. Although I'm easily the youngest person in the room at my classes, I've been accepted as one of them, and I've already been invited back to teach again next semester.

I've been introduced as an "exciting new author" but never "a fresh, new face."

Even in this, my new career, which is only a couple years old, I'm not regarded as the youth of today.

But there's been no attempt by time, events, age, or coincidence to erase me there just yet.

Too Much

If you don't recognize, or remember, the song titles mentioned in this story, listen to them on YouTube or Spotify for a richer reading experience.

A few things before this story gets going. First, it doesn't really belong in this book. It has nothing to do with education or school. I'm only placing it here, near the end of the book, to show you that the things that happened to me at school aren't limited to school. They happen to me at home too. Second, you need to know that my wife and I love our next-door neighbours. They are "finest kind." We wouldn't trade them for anybody. Third, I asked Ken for permission to publish this. He agreed. That's the kind of guy he is. Finest kind, like I said. And fourth, like me, things seem to just *happen* to Ken.

For example, if we're sitting in one of our backyards trading stories, and I tell Ken and Deb about the time flames shot out of the front of a barbecue at my *face*, burning off an inch of my beard, along with my eyebrows and part of the hair on my head, we'll all laugh. Then Ken will tell us about the time flames shot out of the front of *his* barbecue, melting the bathing suit he was wearing to the point that all he had on, *in front of his in-laws*, was the mesh underwear underneath most bathing suits these days.

And we'll laugh and laugh. (Ken wants me to add that he returned that barbecue, which was twelve years old when it melted his trunks, and was given a brand-new one for his embarrassment. "I showed them all that was left of my bathing suit. They were appalled!")

Occasionally, the stories he tells involve the neighbour-hood, like mine do. One day in September, when Linda and I were out of town at a wedding, Ken cleaned out his garage. When we returned, not even twenty-four hours later, Deb, his wife, met us in the driveway and said, "You missed all the excitement!" And then Ken joined her, and it took us only a second to notice that something was different about the way Ken looked.

They told us the story together, like two sports announcers for a baseball game. Deb adding details, sort of colour commentary. I'm sorry we weren't there as witnesses, but hearing Ken and Deb tell the story was almost as good.

As Ken was cleaning out his garage, he found a supply of gunpowder he'd used when he was a disc jockey in the 1980s. He explained that there are two colours of disc jockey–grade gunpowder they use for pyrotechnics: red and black. Red burns slowly, kind of like you've seen in Road Runner cartoons. Black burns far more quickly and creates a lot of smoke. Ken found he had a small supply of both.

To entertain his pre-teen son, and the neighbours, he poured the contents of the red powder along the curb outside his house, creating a thin line about ten feet long. When he ensured that his son was standing a safe distance away, he lit the end of the line, creating the effect we've all witnessed Wile E. Coyote create trying to capture the Road Runner, the flames snaking crazily down the curb.

Ken's son, and the neighbourhood kids, now assembled to watch, applauded like crazy.

Ken then created a similar line of powder but with the remaining black powder, again ensuring that his son was standing a safe distance away before lighting it.

I don't know whether the nurse and doctor at the hospital laughed and laughed when Ken explained how his beard and eyebrows had been burned away, like mine had been by the barbecue from my story. But once we were sure that Ken was fine, and that there was no lasting damage done, we all laughed and laughed.

Anyway, Ken's lived next door to us the whole time we've lived where we live now. We get along very well. He's louder than we are though. He likes his yard tools and power tools to be loud too. *Occasionally,* he uses them at times we find inconvenient, but if we point that out to him, he'll stop.

"Ken! We have my parents over! Dad's hard of hearing, and he can't hear us over your weed whacking!" I'll shout through the fence.

"Oh! Sorry! I'll finish up later. I didn't realize."

He listens to his music a bit louder than we'd like too. There are a few reasons for this: Ken, like my dad, is a bit hard of hearing. Not nearly as bad as my father, but he *is* hard of hearing. Ken was a DJ in his youth, so he's used to listening to his music a bit louder than we do. But the major reason that his music is louder than we'd like is that the music is, well, not really music that we like to listen to.

Please understand. It's not that the music is bad. Our tastes are just different, that's all; for example, Andy Kim's "Rock Me Gently" isn't one of my favourite songs.

When Ken was a DJ, I'm sure that Mr. Kim was a very popular guy, and "Rock Me Gently" was a very popular tune. In fact, I know that. But I've never really liked it. Not in 1974, when it came out, and not at any time since then. A lot of the music that Ken listens to, loudly, is like that. Popular with a lot of people, then and now, but not with me.

Usually, it's not a big deal. He listens to enough stuff that I do like, that I don't mind at all when the occasional "Gone, Gone, Gone" by Chilliwack comes on. (For the record, I do like that song every once in a while.) And sometimes, I actually *do* like the songs, like "December" by Collective Soul, which he played again and again and again one summer.

One summer, though, Ken and I spent far more time in our backyards than usual, at the same time, so I had to listen to more of Ken's music than usual. I must have been building my shed or a porch, expanding the garden or something, so going into the house or into the front yard wasn't an option. Ken had just installed an incredible sound system in his backyard, one fit for a former DJ and one that matched the system in his house. This was at a time when large speakers were a sign of a great sound system, and Ken had had us in to show them to us. Large speakers in rosewood cabinets sat on his fireplace mantel the way flower vases graced ours.

A couple weeks earlier, Ken had left home to go to the grocery store or the car parts store but left his music on outside, I'm sure for the benefit of the neighbourhood, but one of the CDs started skipping. I can't think of too many things more annoying than a CD skipping, loudly, while you're trying to eat lunch with guests, so after a couple minutes, I went over and snipped the wires to the speakers.

When Ken got home, I explained what I'd done and why. Before Ken could apologize or get upset with me, Gino, the neighbour on the other side of Ken's house, shouted over, "If Garlick hadn't snipped the wires when he did, I would've snipped them about ten seconds later! I had the scissors in my hand, Ken!"

Although I was pretty sure Ken had forgiven me for this, as I'd forgiven him for leaving home when a CD was about to start skipping, we hadn't talked about it since.

And the music was back to being too loud again.

"Magic Power" by Triumph was playing, and we could hear it through our closed kitchen windows.

"Do you think if I ask him to turn it down for a bit, he'd turn it down?" I asked Linda.

"That's pretty rude. He's in his own back yard, listening to his own music. It's the summer, and he's in the pool with his kids. Suck it up," Linda advised me.

"That's it! Thanks, hon!"

"What? What did I say?"

I had just bought the Dave Mathews Band's album *Crash* and was particularly enamoured with the song "Too Much," which has a great baritone sax part. Google it, you'll thank me. It was new enough that I didn't think Ken would have heard it yet. "Suck it up" is one of the lyrics.

When I went outside with the CD, Terry Jacks was singing "Seasons in the Sun."

"Hey! Ken! Have you heard this yet?" I shouted over the lyrics. "I think you might like it." I waved the CD. "Do us both a favour and crank this up. Start with 'Too Much.' It kicks!"

I spoke like that back then.

Ken took it into his house. I started hammering, digging, drilling, or whatever I'd been doing, and soon, we, along with many other people in the neighbourhood, were listening to the Dave Mathews Band's "Too Much."

For about three minutes, everything was great, from my perspective. I was whistling while I worked and listening to a kickin' baritone sax.

And then the music stopped. Abruptly.

I guess Ken didn't like it, I thought. Oh well . . .

About five minutes later, Ken came out with my CD and handed it to me through the fence.

"Not your cup of tea, I guess?" I asked.

"No. I really liked it. I guess that 'Too Much' was just too much, or too loud."

"I don't understand."

"That song made my speakers walk off the mantel! They crashed to the floor!"

Although I didn't get to hear *my* music outside that summer, I didn't have to listen to Ken's music either.

Heaven for a Teacher

The band has taken a break, and while they were excellent, one of the best bands you've heard in a very long time, you appreciate the quiet that's replaced them. You take a sip from your drink and look around the place for the first time since you sat down. It's then that you notice them.

They sit in a quiet, dimly lit corner of the quiet, dimly lit pub, this man and woman.

From where you're sitting, you can't tell how old he might be. He's one of those men who has been accused of "having a picture in the attic," and former students have often said, "Sir! My God! It's been *years*! You look exactly the same!"

He knows that's never really been true. The beard is much whiter, the hair thinner, and if you look around his eyes, you can see the wrinkles formed by decades and decades of smiling and laughing. But it's never around his eyes that you look. It's into his eyes. They sparkle the way you remember when you said, "Hey, sir!" to him in the hall, or when he told you that silly horse joke in class, or when you asked if you could hug him the day you graduated.

And her? Well, she could be *any* age. When you first saw her, you thought she was maybe old enough to be your mother. Looking again, perhaps just an older sister or aunt. And when she laughs, she might even be a bit younger than you. If you do see a streak of grey hair, you'd think it was there by design, put there to make her look more mature than she really is. Someone who would catch the eye of the man she's talking with.

But she isn't the one doing the talking. The man—he's the one monopolizing the conversation.

You think, Let her talk, Pops. You're gonna drive her away if you don't let her take part in this.

She doesn't look bored though. A great actress, you think. She'll let him go on and on, and have a pleasant enough evening, let him think he's getting somewhere, and then, when the evening's over, well, a good time was had by all, right?

He's stopped for a minute to sip from his wine. And to think back.

"Let's see . . . I'm forty-six, no forty-seven. I've been teaching more than half my life, and I'm finally comfortable being asked for parenting advice by the parents of kids who are doing really well at school but not so well at home. I'm now the same age, if not older than these parents. I tell them, 'What works for me won't necessarily work for you. I treat Jimmy like an adult; like a potential friend.' Or, 'I give Hussein responsibilities in the school. Things that people depend on him for. He never fails to impress.' 'Janey doesn't need any extra pressure from me. She puts it all on herself. I just make sure she knows that it's okay to mess up occasionally.' The parents look at me like I've dropped gold nuggets in their laps. Secrets of the ages. And then a few weeks later I get thanks from both the kids and the parents."

He takes another sip from his glass. "This may be the best wine I've ever had. You said it's local?"

"Yes. It's made right around here."

"It reminds me of one of the wines my wife and I tried on a tour in Niagara. But that must have been . . ." The man stops and looks sad for a moment.

She smiles. "She'll be joining us in a little while, right?"

"I hope so! I told her I'd be waiting for her here."

So, the old guy is not trying to make time with the younger woman. *Is* she younger than he is? She's certainly attractive, though. It's hard to take your eyes off her, even when the man is talking. And maybe now you can understand her attention to him. Maybe he *is* dropping gold nuggets.

"No! I'm fifty! I remember that it's just before my birthday when I get a call from a former student named Nicole. She had really struggled in school. She'd actually been kicked out before she landed in my class. I don't know what I said or did, but I connected with her, you know? She ended up with the highest mark in my class and graduated with a full ride to—Fanshawe, I think. She was just calling to thank me and tell me that she doesn't know where she'd be if I hadn't come along. Fifteen years after she'd graduated high school. She started crying when I said that of course I remembered her, and then I started crying too.

"Twenty-three was fine too. First days of teaching. Getting *paid* to do what I would gladly have done for free.

"My retirement party was a blast. I remember one of my favourite VPs coming up to me, telling me she'd just gotten word she'd been promoted for the coming school year. Sort of a changing of the guard.

"And in the time since then, writing all these stories. It's too hard for me to decide which was best . . ."

She smiles again. "Perhaps I wasn't being clear, Dave. You don't have to decide. You get them all, whenever you want, and so much more."

Now it's Dave's turn to smile. "No. You were clear. I understood. I was just trying to make you understand. Even with not having to choose, the choices will be difficult. Which would come first?"

And then an even bigger smile.

"Here she is! I knew she'd be here!"

For some reason, you would have guessed she was with him if you'd had the time, but she was suddenly next to him at the table. When he stands up to kiss her, it brings you the same joy it always brings to see a couple who has been together for a lifetime and are obviously as deeply in love as the day they married.

"*This* place?" she says with a smile on her face. Despite her words, you can tell she's pleased with the choice.

"It's where we met. And I told you I'd see you here."

"Yes, I know, but you could have chosen any place. Any place at all." She turns her attention to the woman. It seems as though they are at least acquainted. Maybe friends.

"Thank you for keeping my husband company. I hope he hasn't been bending your ear too much. And in *this* place. He could have at least chosen someplace *new*."

"Yes. But we have an eternity to explore those places now. I thought it best to start here, where we started the first time. What would you like me to order for you? The wine is exceptional, but I get the idea that anything you want will be wonderful."

The young, or old—it doesn't really matter—woman stands up. "I'll leave the two of you now. You have a little catching up to do. It hasn't really been that long though. You two are doing—will do—just fine. Remember though, both and each of you, whenever you want, wherever you want. Forever."